Daniel Veysie

The Doctrine of Atonement Illustrated and Defended

In eight sermons, preached before the University of Oxford in the year 1795

Daniel Veysie

The Doctrine of Atonement Illustrated and Defended
In eight sermons, preached before the University of Oxford in the year 1795

ISBN/EAN: 9783337087913

Printed in Europe, USA, Canada, Australia, Japan

Cover: Foto ©Lupo / pixelio.de

More available books at **www.hansebooks.com**

THE
DOCTRINE of ATONEMENT

ILLUSTRATED AND DEFENDED,

IN

EIGHT SERMONS,

PREACHED BEFORE THE

UNIVERSITY OF OXFORD,

IN THE YEAR 1795,

AT THE

LECTURE FOUNDED BY

The late Rev. JOHN BAMPTON, M. A.

CANON OF SALISBURY.

By DANIEL VEYSIE, B.D.

FELLOW OF ORIEL COLLEGE,

AND ONE OF HIS MAJESTY'S PREACHERS AT WHITEHALL.

OXFORD:

PRINTED FOR FLETCHER AND HANWELL; AND FOR LEIGH AND SOTHEBY, YORK-STREET, COVENT GARDEN, LONDON.

M DCC XCV.

IMPRIMATUR,

JOHAN. WILLS,
VICE-CAN.

Wadh. Coll.
20mo die Junii, 1795.

TO

THE RIGHT REVEREND

AND REVEREND

THE HEADS OF COLLEGES

IN THE

UNIVERSITY OF OXFORD,

THE

FOLLOWING SERMONS,

PREACHED BY THEIR APPOINTMENT,

ARE MOST RESPECTFULLY

INSCRIBED.

EXTRACT

FROM THE

LAST WILL AND TESTAMENT

OF THE LATE

REV. JOHN BAMPTON,

CANON OF SALISBURY.

———" I give and bequeath my Lands and
" Eſtates to the Chancellor, Maſters, and
" Scholars of the Univerſity of Oxford for
" ever, to have and to hold all and ſingular
" the ſaid Lands or Eſtates upon truſt, and to
" the intents and purpoſes hereinafter men-
" tioned; that is to ſay, I will and appoint
" that the Vice-Chancellor of the Univerſity
" of Oxford for the time being ſhall take and
" receive

" receive all the rents, issues, and profits
" thereof, and (after all taxes, reparations
" and necessary deductions made) that he
" pay all the remainder to the endowment
" of eight Divinity Lecture Sermons, to be
" established for ever in the said Univer-
" sity, and to be performed in the manner
" following:

" I direct and appoint, that, upon the first
" Tuesday in Easter Term, a Lecturer be
" yearly chosen by the Heads of Colleges
" only, and by no others, in the room ad-
" joining to the Printing-House, between
" the hours of ten in the morning and two
" in the afternoon, to preach eight Divinity
" Lecture Sermons, the year following, at St.
" Mary's in Oxford, between the commence-
" ment of the last month in Lent Term, and
" the end of the third week in Act Term.

" Also I direct and appoint, that the eight
" Divinity Lecture Sermons shall be preached
" upon either of the following subjects—to
" confirm and establish the Christian Faith,
" and

" and to confute all heretics and fchifmatics
" —upon the divine authority of the Holy
" Scriptures — upon the authority of the
" writings of the primitive Fathers, as to
" the faith and practice of the primitive
" Church—upon the Divinity of our Lord
" and Saviour Jefus Chrift—upon the Di-
" vinity of the Holy Ghoft—upon the Ar-
" ticles of the Chriftian Faith, as compre-
" hended in the Apoftles' and Nicene
" Creeds.

" Alfo I direct, that thirty copies of the
" eight Divinity Lecture Sermons fhall be
" always printed, within two months after
" they are preached, and one copy fhall be
" given to the Chancellor of the Univerfity,
" and one copy to the Head of every Col-
" lege, and one copy to the Mayor of the
" city of Oxford, and one copy to be put
" into the Bodleian Library; and the ex-
" pence of printing them fhall be paid out
" of the revenue of the Land or Eftates given
" for eftablifhing the Divinity Lecture Ser-
" mons; and the Preacher fhall not be paid,
" nor

" nor be entitled to the revenue, before they
" are printed.

" Alfo I direct and appoint, that no per-
" fon fhall be qualified to preach the Divi-
" nity Lecture Sermons, unlefs he hath taken
" the Degree of Mafter of Arts at leaft, in
" one of the two Univerfities of Oxford or
" Cambridge; and that the fame perfon
" fhall never preach the Divinity Lecture
" Sermons twice."

SERMON I.

1 Tim. ii. 5.

There is one God and one Mediator between God and Men, the Man Christ Jesus.

BELIEF in God is the foundation of all religion, both natural and revealed. And as there never was a people so barbarous as to have lost all sense of religion, so there never was a people among whom the notion of a God was entirely obliterated. Even in the lowest state of intellectual degeneracy mankind have still retained some apprehension of a supernatural Power, whose intervention and invisible agency they have invariably acknowledged, as often as events occurred for which they could not account by natural means, or effects were produced for which they could not assign any visible cause. And wherever the faculties of the human mind

mind have been cultivated and improved, there has generally prevailed a full perfuafion of a great firft Caufe, from whofe creative power all things derived their origin, and by whofe fuperintending Providence they are governed and upheld. Indeed fo conftant and univerfal has been the belief of all mankind in the exiftence of a Deity, that it has by fome been imagined to be a principle natural to the mind of man, and born in him. But however this be, we may venture at leaft to affirm, that it is a truth agreeable to the reafon of man, and muft always meet with a willing affent from every mind, the faculties of which are not naturally defective, or have not been depraved by vice and fenfuality.

That God is one, is a truth which has not been fo univerfally received. Many nations have acknowledged a multiplicity of Deities; and perhaps the unity of the divine nature was never acknowledged by any nation, which had not been in fome degree illuminated with the rays of divine light. At one period of the world it was the profeffed belief of only a fingle people, who at that very time were under the immediate care and direction

rection of Heaven, and were favoured with positive declarations of the Divine will. And even at present the inhabitants of the unenlightened parts of our globe acknowledge Gods many, and Lords many. And if to us there is but one God, to what shall we attribute our knowledge of this truth, but to the revelation which that same God has been pleased to make of his nature and perfections? But this truth, though, as it should seem, not discoverable without revelation, and perhaps even now not reducible to any first principle, yet, being revealed, strongly recommends itself to the best reason of mankind, and obtains from the approving mind a ready and entire assent.

From the existence of a great first Cause, we naturally proceed to the relation in which we stand, and the duties which we owe to this divine Being. As well as the Creator, he is the Lord and Governor of the universe; and as such may justly claim from all his creatures and subjects adoration and worship; an entire submission to the dispensations of his Providence, and an unreserved obedience to the expressions of his will. He is also our Father and Protector, upon whom we depend for preservation and support, and from whom must proceed the supply of our wants. He is therefore justly entitled to our reverence and love; to our praise for past instances of bounty, and to our prayers for the things of which we stand in need.

But God is the great King of all the earth, and no less glorious in purity than in greatness: we are sinful dust and ashes. How then will he deign to hold communion with us, or how shall we presume to appear before him? This sense of man's unworthiness, when compared with the Divine majesty and holiness, seems little less familiar to the human mind than the belief of God's existence. And therefore in all ages men, dreading the immediate presence of the Deity, have sought the interposition of Mediators and Intercessors, by whose ministry all intercourse might be carried on between the great objects of their worship and themselves. Thus the Heathens formed to themselves a crowd of Mediators—beings of a middle order—to whom they assigned the office of presenting to the Gods the addresses of men, and of communicating to men the favours of the Gods. And this mode of communication has

has received the sanction of the true God; who ordained his covenant with the Israelites in the hand of a Mediator, viz. Moses; through whom he made known to the people his statutes and judgments. And much after the same manner the people performed to God the religious worship and service which their law prescribed. For they were not permitted to stand before God, and perform in person the rites of their religion; but were commanded to have recourse to the mediation of their Priests, through whom they presented their addresses and offerings of blood, and from whose interposition they were taught to expect the divine favour and acceptance.

Nor was the New Covenant established without a Mediator. For as " there is one God," so there is " one Mediator between God and Men." And it was to appear in this character for the salvation of a sinful world, that the divine Word, the second person of the ever-blessed Trinity, divested himself of that glory which he had with the Father before the foundation of the world, even from all eternity, and condescended to take upon him our flesh, and to become man. For the

Apostle,

Apoſtle, having aſſerted that there is one Mediator between God and men, immediately adds, that this Mediator is " the Man Chriſt Jeſus."

From what has been ſaid, it appears that the mediatorial character implies at leaſt two diſtinct offices, uſually denominated the *prophetical* and the *ſacerdotal*; and that a Mediator is either a Prophet or a Prieſt, according as he is commiſſioned to act, either in the name of God for the purpoſe of declaring his will to mankind, or in behalf of men for the purpoſe of recommending them to the favour of God. Now the mediatorial character of Chriſt has been generally underſtood to include both theſe offices; and accordingly Chriſt has uſually been accounted both a Prophet and a Prieſt: a Prophet, or the Ambaſſador of God to men; a Prieſt, or the Advocate of men with God. To theſe principal, and, if I may ſo ſpeak, eſſential branches of the mediatorial character, Divines, upon the authority of the Scriptures, have added a third; viz. the *regal*; to which our Lord Jeſus Chriſt was admitted after his aſcenſion into heaven, as the reward of his ſufferings upon earth, and for the benefit of that

Church

Church which he had purchased with his blood.

Nor is it without reason that the name *Christ,* which answers to the Hebrew *Messiah,* and signifies *anointed,* has been thought to indicate the three offices above-mentioned. For as under the law the ceremony of anointing was by God's own appointment the mode of consecration to the three offices of Prophet, Priest, and King; so was Christ also anointed, not indeed with material oil, but with the spiritual unction of the Holy Ghost, to be the Prophet, Priest, and King of his people. He is their Prophet, to declare the will of God, and to make known the way of salvation; he is their Priest, to interpose in their behalf, and by an offering of his own blood to procure for them a favourable acceptance in the sight of God; and he is their King, to distribute among them his manifold gifts of grace during their continuance in this lower world, and to conduct them to ever-enduring mansions of glory in the world to come.

Of these offices the prophetical and regal are universally acknowledged. There never existed a sect of Christians, hardy enough to deny that Christ was that Prophet which should come into the world; or that after having declared the will of God, and finished the work which was given him to do, he afcended up on high far above all heavens; angels, and authorities and powers being made fubject unto him ª. But his facerdotal office,

---

ª Socinus and his immediate followers were ftrenuous advocates for the regal office, affirming that by virtue of this office Chrift was invefted with the power of delivering his people from the punifhment of fin. Modern Socinians indeed betray an inclination to deprive the Saviour of the regal as well as the facerdotal character, and to reduce him to the condition of a mere Prophet. This I infer from an obfervation which occurs in the Hiftory of the Corruptions of Chriftianity, vol. i. p. 272; where the Author, fpeaking of the above opinion of Socinus, has the following words:
" Fauftus Socinus, who diftinguifhed himfelf fo much in
" recovering the original doctrine of the proper *humanity*
" *of Chrift*, as to give occafion to all who now hold that
" doctrine to be called by his name, faw clearly the abfur-
" dity of what was advanced by the other reformers con-
" cerning fatisfaction being made to the juftice of God by
" the death of Chrift. Indeed it immediately follows from
" his principles, that Chrift being only a man, though ever
" fo innocent, his death could not, in any proper fenfe
" of the word, atone for the fins of other men. He was
" however far from abandoning the doctrine of *redemption*
" in the Scripture fenfe of the word, that is, of our deliver-
" ance from the guilt of fin by his Gofpel, as promoting
" repentance and reformation, and from the punifhment
" due to fin, by his power of giving eternal life to all that
" obey him. *But, indeed, if God himfelf freely forgives the*
" *fins*

SERMON I.

office, that office upon the difcharge of which our hopes of life and falvation are principally founded, has unhappily not been fo univerfally acknowledged. There are not wanting men who receive not Chrift as their Prieft, and who difown any immediate virtue in his death to obtain remiffion of fins, and to procure for us God's favour and acceptance.

It is eafy to perceive that they who thus deny the Prieftly office of our Redeemer, do in effect deny the whole fcheme of Redemption, as held by our Church, or rather by the univerfal Church of Chrift. In modern times this denial conftitutes a diftinguifhing article in the creed of an heretical fect, called, after the name of its founder, *the Socinian*; which firft appeared about the time of the reformation from Popery, and has continued ever fince to infeft the Church. In our own nation the opinions of this fect have never, from the very firft, wanted advocates and abettors; and of late have been moft ftrenuoufly afferted by a writer of very confiderable eminence, in a well-known work, entitled

" *fins of men upon their repentance, there could be no occa-*
" *fion, properly fpeaking, for any thing farther being done to*
" *avert the punifhment with which they had been threat-*
" *ened,*"

" A Hiftory

SERMON I.

"A History of the Corruptions of Christianity." Among these corruptions the doctrine of Atonement has obtained a principal place. In point of order it ranks the second; for the history of this doctrine immediately succeeds that of opinions relating to Jesus Christ: and in point of importance it is esteemed by the historian himself inferior to none; as is apparent from the manner in which it is introduced to the notice of his readers. "As," says he, "the doctrine of the divine Unity was infringed by the introduction of that of the Divinity of Christ and of the Holy Ghost (as a person distinct from the Father), so the doctrine of the natural placability of the divine Being, and our ideas of the equity of his government, have been greatly debased by the gradual introduction of the modern doctrine of Atonement [b]." And presently after he tells us, that he conceives this doctrine to be a gross misrepresentation of the character and moral government of God, and to affect many other articles in the scheme of Christianity, greatly disfiguring and depraving it; and therefore he declares his intention of shewing, in a fuller manner than he means to do with

[b] Hist. of Cor. vol. i. p. 152.

respect

SERMON I.

respect to any other corruption of Christianity, that it has no countenance whatever in reason or the Scriptures, and that the whole doctrine, with every modification of it, has been a departure from the primitive and genuine doctrine of Christianity [e].

To an unprejudiced mind it must occasion no little surprize, that a doctrine, which, by the confession of this author, is become in a manner universal, and has taken the firmest hold upon men's minds, should have thus creeped in, and prevailed without the least countenance either from reason or from the Scriptures: and it behoves us to receive with caution, and to examine with care, whatever is advanced in support of so bold an assertion. That the doctrine, if true, is of the greatest importance, will not be denied; since it concerns nothing less than the foundation upon which are built all our hopes of paying to God an acceptable service in this life, and of being admitted to the everlasting enjoyment of him in the life to come. Persuaded myself of its truth, I shall offer no apology for an humble, but honest, attempt, to illustrate and defend it; nor do I know in what other

[e] Hist. of Cor. p. 153.

way

way I can employ the ability which God hath given me more advantageously to the cause of religion, or more agreeably to the intention of the Founder of this Lecture.

The doctrine of Atonement, then, is the subject of which I propose to treat, and I trust I shall be able to shew, in opposition to the writer above referred to, that it is contained in the Scriptures, and that the arguments by which it is assailed are in general inconclusive, and not unfrequently wholly inapplicable to the point in question. And because in every controversy it is of the utmost consequence to ascertain and determine what this point is, in order to remove as much as possible all occasion of misconception and erroneous judgment, those copious sources of objection and dispute, it is my design, in the remaining part of this discourse, to prepare the way for the due investigation of the subject before us, by stating the doctrine in its plain and simple form, divested of every circumstance in which the issue of the controversy is not immediately concerned.

And in order to this it will be necessary, in the first place, to ascertain the scriptural meaning of the term *atonement*.

SERMON I.

To be at one, is an obsolete form of speech, signifying *to be reconciled*, or to *come to an agreement after having been at variance*. And accordingly *atonement*, which by Etymologists is derived from hence, properly signifies *agreement* or *reconciliation*[d]: and in this its primitive sense, which was antiently its common and usual one, it is uniformly taken in our translation of the Scriptures. In the Old Testament it is frequently used with reference to the legal sin-offerings, with the blood of which the Priest is said to *make an atonement*. The original word used on these occasions, which for the most part is thus translated, is also occasionally rendered *to reconcile*; a strong presumption that our Translators annexed to both expressions the same meaning. Thus in the sixteenth chapter of Leviticus, the High Priest, on the great day of expiation, is commanded to sprinkle the blood of the sin-offerings, and to *make an atonement for the holy place*; and presently after this very act is called *reconciling* the holy place[e]. In the original the word in both

[d] See Francisci Junii Etymologicum Anglicanum, and Skinner's Etymologicon Linguæ Anglicanæ. See also authorities for this use of the word, drawn from the earlier English writers, in Johnson's Dictionary.
[e] Lev. xvi. 16, 20.

places is the fame; viz. כפר : as it is alfo in the Septuagint, viz. εξιλασκομαι, *to appeafe* or *make propitious*; which word, for the moſt part, correfponds to *making atonement* in our verſion. In the New Teſtament the term *atonement* occurs but once; and then it unqueſtionably ſignifies *reconciliation*. It is in the following paſſage from St. Paul's Epiſtle to the Romans. "For if when we were "enemies we were reconciled ($\kappa\alpha\tau\eta\lambda\lambda\alpha\gamma\eta\mu\epsilon\nu$) "to God by the death of his Son, much "more being reconciled ($\kappa\alpha\tau\alpha\lambda\lambda\alpha\gamma\epsilon\nu\tau\epsilon\varsigma$) we "ſhall be faved by his life. And not only "ſo, but we alfo joy in God through our "Lord Jefus Chriſt, by whom we have now "received the atonement ($\kappa\alpha\tau\alpha\lambda\lambda\alpha\gamma\eta\nu$)[f]" *i. e.* the reconciliation; as the word had twice before been rendered in this very paſſage. From all which it is manifeſt, that the ſcriptural meaning of *atonement* is *reconciliation*; and accordingly to affert of Chriſt that he hath *made an atonement for us* by his blood, is the fame as to affert that he hath *reconciled us to God* by his blood; or, in other words, that by his death he hath made God propitious to ſinful man, and hath procured for all who believe in him pardon and acceptance.

[f] Rom. v. 10.

And

SERMON I.

And this propofition contains, as I conceive, all that is effential to the doctrine of Atonement. It has indeed been ufual to ftate the doctrine in a fuller manner, fo as not fimply to affert our reconciliation to God by the blood of Chrift, but alfo to fuperadd the ground and reafon of the reconciliation. And this addition, derived not fo much from the pofitive declarations of Scripture, as from the views which men have entertained of the fubject, and their reafonings refpecting it, has been fo generally acquiefced in and acknowledged, that it is commonly fuppofed to be infeparably connected with the doctrine, and to conftitute a neceffary and effential part of it. But however true in itfelf, it has unfortunately occafioned much mifreprefentation and unjuft cenfure, and (as we fhall fee in the fequel) has been the foundation of moft of the principal objections againft the doctrine itfelf. It is therefore become highly ufeful, and even neceffary, to feparate from the real queftion this and every other adventitious circumftance with which it has been ufually implicated.

It has perhaps already occurred to every one who hears me, that the circumftance to which I principally refer, as an addition to the

the pure and simple doctrine of atonement, or reconciliation by the death of Christ, is the following; viz. that Christ died to make satisfaction to the divine justice. Now the sacred writers no where, as far as I know, expressly assert any satisfaction at all as having been effected by the death of Christ. At the same time it must be acknowledged, that the generality of Christians, in modern times at least, have concurred in maintaining as abovementioned, that by the death of Christ satisfaction was made to the justice of God; and so universal has been this concurrence, that the *doctrine of Satisfaction* has been commonly used as a synonimous expression for the *doctrine of Atonement*. Divines of our own country may probably have been confirmed in this use of the term, by its common acceptation. For though it was antiently taken, in what is still its sole scriptural sense, to signify *reconciliation*, yet because reconciliations are for the most part brought about by the aggressor's making satisfaction for his wrong by the payment of an equivalent to the party aggrieved, therefore in process of time *atonement* came to signify *compensation* and *satisfaction*; and men accustomed to this use of the term may have been led to imagine that the work

work of Chrift for our redemption, was undertaken with a view to fomething of this kind. But from whatever caufe it has arifen, certain it is, that the death of Chrift has been called and accounted not merely a *propitiation*, or that on account of which God is become merciful to man, and man acceptable to God; but further, a *fatisfaction*. And this fatisfaction is fuppofed to have been required in confequence of that violation of the divine law, and that difobedience to the divine authority, which occafioned the fall of man. And fince the fatisfaction muft of courfe be made to God, whofe law was broken, and whofe authority was difobeyed, to what attribute of the Deity could it with fuch propriety be afcribed as to his juftice, which feems efpecially concerned to vindicate the honour of the divine law, and to inflict upon offenders the due reward of their evil deeds?

Concerning this fatisfaction to the juftice of God, there have been principally two opinions. And firft, fome, and thofe Divines of great learning and piety, have contended for the abfolute neceffity of fuch a fatisfaction, in order to maintain the inviolability of the Divine attributes. For they argue that fin is fo oppofite to the purity and holinefs of God,

C and

and of confequence fo odious in his fight that it cannot but provoke his difpleafure, and expofe all who commit it to his wrath and indignation. And fince juftice is effential to the Divine nature, and exifts there in a fupreme degree, it muft inflexibly require the punifhment of thofe who are thus the objects of wrath : nor is it poffible that the punifhment due to fin could have been remitted, if fatisfaction had not been made to the juftice of God. Hence they conclude, that fuch fatisfaction was actually made by Jefus Chrift ; whofe death, being an equivalent for that of the whole human race, obtained our acquittal, and laid the foundation of our title to eternal life.

Others, in the fecond place, not contending for the abfolute neceffity of a fatisfaction to Divine juftice, infift only upon the wifdom and fitnefs of the meafure : and fuch conſider God in the light of a Governor, or Judge, who for the direction of his fubjects had given them an exprefs law, and had fanctioned it by denouncing pofitive punifhment againft all who fhould tranfgrefs it. Now, fay they, it unqueftionably became the Almighty Sovereign and Governor of the univerfe to confult the honour of his law, and

not

SERMON I.

not to suffer it to be violated with impunity, or without satisfaction, lest the subjects of his authority should be induced to call in question his justice, and to vilify and set at nought his office of Judge. Willing, therefore, to shew mercy to his offending creatures, but unwilling that his forbearance of punishment should endanger the ends of his government, he was pleased to ordain a propitiation for sin. Accordingly he sent into the world his own Son, who, by dying for our sins, obtained our release from all obligation to punishment, while at the same time he made a most glorious display of the righteousness of God. And thus, it is contended, by the appointment of Jesus Christ to be a propitiation, satisfaction was made for sin: the Divine law was satisfied; *i. e.* its claim was silenced, and the sinner was no longer exposed to its rigour: the Divine justice was also satisfied; *i. e.* it no longer required that the punishment due to sin should be inflicted upon the offender. In a word, according to this opinion, Christ is said to have made satisfaction for our sins, not because his death is to be accounted an adequate compensation, or a full equivalent; but because his suffering in our stead maintained the honour of the Divine law, and gave free scope to the mercy of the Lawgiver, without any impeachment or diminution of his justice. And satisfaction, in this qualified sense, has been commonly received among Divines; and especially is maintained by Grotius, in his celebrated treatise against Socinus, expressly entitled " De Satisfactione Christi;" and also by Stillingfleet, in his able defence of Grotius against the subtleties of Crellius; both of whom consider God not as a party aggrieved or offended, demanding full amends and adequate compensation for the wrong he had suffered; but as a wise and prudent Governor, requiring such a satisfaction as he might deem necessary for maintaining the authority of his laws, and for enabling him to extend mercy to criminals, without giving encouragement to crime, or in any respect endangering the purposes of government.

Which of these opinions is true, or whether either of them be true, I am not called upon to determine; for neither of them is essential to the doctrine of Atonement: and could it even be proved that both of them are false, the real question would not be at all affected. I cannot however refrain from a few observations, by way of reply to those

harsh

harsh and unmerited censures, to which the doctrine, considered under this view, has unhappily given rise.

I have already had occasion to bring forward an assertion, made by our Opponent at the very commencement of the history with which we are at present concerned; viz. that " the doctrine of the natural placability of " the divine Being, and our ideas of the " equity of his government, have been greatly " debased by the introduction of the doctrine " of Atonement." The ground upon which he hazards this assertion is, that this latter doctrine " represents the divine Being as " *withholding* his mercy from the *truly peni-* " *tent*, till a *full* satisfaction be made to his " justice." Were this indeed the case, there would, apparently at least, be some foundation for the charge, that the doctrine of Atonement debases the natural placability, and misrepresents the character and moral government of God. For rigidly to demand satisfaction for an offence, and, notwithstanding the repentance of the offender, still to continue implacable till the required satisfaction be made, seems to be the part of a merciless and resentful Being, rather than of a benevolent and compassionate God, such as is the

God revealed to us in the holy Scriptures. But this is not the cafe. On the other hand, the charge thus brought againſt the doctrine of Atonement is founded upon a grofs mif-ſtatement of the fentiments of Believers refpecting this doctrine, to whom no fuch reprefentation of the divine Being, as is here fuppofed, can juſtly be imputed. Indeed it is not pretended that this reprefentation can be inferred, except from the opinion of thofe who contend for a full fatisfaction to the juſtice of God, which, as I before obferved, is far from being the univerfal opinion. Nor can it fairly be inferred even from this opinion. For they who affert a fatisfaction in its moſt rigid fenfe, ſtill contend, that this fatisfaction was made, or at leaſt decreed, according to fome, from the very foundation of the world; and at furtheſt immediately after the fall, when as yet man was hardly fenfible of his fin and folly. And therefore, even under this view of the doctrine, God cannot be faid to *withhold* mercy from the truly penitent, when he was pleafed to open a way for the exercife of his mercy, by the fatisfaction of his juſtice, before any repentance on the part of man could poſſibly have taken place. In truth, the doctrine of Atonement,

under

under whatever view we confider it, is fo far from debafing, that it moft powerfully confirms and eftablifhes the placability of the Deity. It reprefents not God as a refentful Being, but as full of mercy and compaffion—not vindictively demanding fatisfaction; but gracioufly appointing a propitiation—not withholding mercy from the truly penitent; but even anticipating man's repentance, and when we were enemies to him, freely providing the means of our reconciliation, and fending his Son to die for our fins [g].

There is a further mifreprefentation of the fentiments of Believers in the ftatement which our Hiftorian has given, of the manner in which the doctrine of Atonement is connected with that of the divinity of Jefus Chrift. In contending for this connection, we are fuppofed to argue after the following manner. " Sin being an offence againft an
" infinite Being, requires an infinite fatisfac-
" tion, which can only be made by an infi-
" nite perfon; that is, one who is no lefs
" than God himfelf: Chrift therefore, in order
" to make this infinite fatisfaction for the

---

[g] See this fubject further difcuffed in Serm. VI.

SERMON I.

" fins of men, muft himfelf be God, equal to
" the Father [h]." This argument, as it proceeds upon the fuppofition that an adequate fatisfaction was required for the fins of mankind, can only be objected againft thofe who are advocates for that opinion; and is therefore unfairly attributed to Believers in general. Indeed, even allowing the foundation upon which it is built, it would ftill be a weak argument, and might eafily be retorted. For with no lefs reafon might it be argued, that fin, being committed by a finite creature, requires only a finite fatisfaction; to the making of which a finite perfon is fully adequate. If fuch an argument for the divinity of Chrift has unwarily fallen from any friend to the doctrine of Atonement, it is to be lamented that it fhould have been hazarded unneceffarily, and without fufficient warrant from Scripture. We believe indeed the divinity of Chrift, becaufe the Scriptures have exprefsly declared it: but we pretend not to infer it from the fuppofed neceffity of an infinite fatisfaction: on the contrary, we infer from it the love of God towards us, of which the appointment of his divine Son to be the

[h] Hift. of Cor. p. 153.

propitiation

propitiation for our fins, is a moft convincing proof; and we build upon it a fure and certain expectation of his future favour. " He that fpared not his own Son, but delivered him up for us all, how fhall he not with him alfo freely give us all things[1]?"

Another circumftance connected by our Hiftorian with the doctrine of Atonement, and made as it were to fpring from it, is, the imputation of Chrift's righteoufnefs to Believers as the ground of their acceptance with God. What was before obferved refpecting fatisfaction to Divine juftice, is alfo true of imputed righteoufnefs; it is no where exprefsly afferted in the facred writings. And although our Hiftorian appears in words to confider it as a neceffary appendage to the doctrine of Atonement, and as univerfally maintained by the advocates of this doctrine; yet he could not be ignorant that the fact is otherwife; and that imputed righteoufnefs is not more a ground of controverfy between thofe who believe the doctrine of Atonement and thofe who do not, than it is between thofe who believe the doctrine among them-

---

[1] Rom. viii. 32.

felves. They who hold imputed righteoufnefs, feem to be of opinion, that, fince Chrift died in order to bear the punifhment of our fins, no higher effect can properly be afcribed to his death, than our deliverance from condemnation. But fomething further is neceffary to reftore us to God's favour; viz. a perfect righteoufnefs. But fince fuch righteoufnefs is not inherent in even the beft of men, it can be ours only by imputation. And hence they argue, that, as by the imputation of our guilt to Chrift we are delivered from the punifhment of fin; fo by the imputation of his righteoufnefs to us we are reftored to the favour of God. But this doctrine, fo ftrongly infifted upon by fome, is, in the eftimation of others, unneceffary in the Chriftian fcheme. It is granted, that, in order to forgivenefs, we muft be cleanfed from the guilt of fin by the blood of Chrift: now they argue, that to thofe who are thus cleanfed, fin is not imputed; that is, in other words, they are accounted righteous; they are in the fight of God, as though they had never offended; and confequently are again become, what, had they continued innocent, they would never have ceafed to be, objects of his love and favour. And thus, according to this argument,

ment, not only pardon, but acceptance also, is the immediate effect of Chrift's death.

I am not concerned to fhew which of thefe opinions is moft confonant to the fpirit and intention of the facred writings. It is fufficient that imputed righteoufnefs, however confiftent with the doctrine of Atonement, is neverthelefs not effential to it, and may therefore be confidered as an addition to the pure and fimple doctrine. And I cannot but obferve, that this or any other doctrine is mifreprefented, when that is affumed as neceffary and effential, which is merely adventitious and accidental; and which, if denied, would ftill leave the genuine doctrine entire and unimpaired.

As it is the profeffed intention of this difcourfe to determine the fcriptural meaning of *atonement*, in order to afcertain the real nature of the doctrine, I think it not improper in this place to animadvert upon the fenfe which our Hiftorian has attempted to affix to this term, as often as it occurs in the Teftament—a fenfe, which, if it could fupported, would entirely exclude eve of propitiation. He tells us, that, "fr. " paring all the paffages in which

"is mentioned, it is evident that it fignifies
"the making of any thing *clean* or *holy*, fo
"as to be fit to be ufed in the fervice of
"God; or, when applied to a *perfon*, fit to
"come into the prefence of God; God
"being confidered as in a peculiar manner
"the King and Sovereign of the Ifraelitifh
"nation, and, as it were, keeping a court
"among them [k]."

That the authority of the Seventy (who, as above ftated, render the original word by εξιλασκομαι, to appeafe or make propitious) is decidedly againft this interpretation, cannot be denied. The truth is, there runs through the whole a miftake, arifing from a partial view of the fubject, and a mifconception of the nature and intention of the legal atonements. That the perfon or thing, for which an atonement was made, was in confequence of the atonement cleanfed, or made holy, and fit for the fervice of God, the Scriptures exprefsly affert. But the efficacy of thefe atonements did not ftop here. The end propofed by them was to recommend and make acceptable to God the things intended for his fervice, which on account of fome

[k] Hift. of Cor. p. 193.

unfitnefs,

unfitness, either natural or acquired, were objects of displeasure rather than of favour. Accordingly atonement implies a double effect; one referring to the *thing*, the other to *God*. With respect to the thing, it implies a removal of the uncleanness which made it an object of displeasure; with respect to God, it implies a removal of the displeasure which the uncleanness had occasioned. The atonement was made *for* the thing, which being in itself unclean and unholy, was in consequence cleansed and sanctified: but it was made *to* God, that he might be reconciled to, and take pleasure in, those things which, in their natural state, were unworthy and unfit for his service. Hence an atonement was made for the altar, when it was originally consecrated [1], and for the Levites, when they were dedicated to their office and ministry [m], in order that, being cleansed from that pollution which naturally cleaves to all terrestrial things, they might become acceptable to God, and fit for his service. In like manner, and for the same reason, atonements were appointed in cases where the uncleanness was contracted: for a house after having been in-

---

[1] Exod. xxix. 36, 37. [m] Num. viii. 12.

fected

fected with leprosy[n]; at the purification of a leper[o]; after involuntary uncleanness[p] and sins of ignorance[q]; as well as in some cases of wilful transgression, upon repentance and restitution[r]. I am ready to allow, and I shall hereafter[s] shew at large, that the atonements in all these cases had no relation to the pardon of sin in a moral sense: that was only to be effected by the atonement made by Christ. I agree that they concerned only the decency and propriety of public worship, qualifying for appearing before God in the earthly tabernacle, and for being employed in his service, for which any thing unclean or polluted was considered as disqualified. Still I contend, that they referred immediately to God, whose favourable acceptance they were intended to procure; and were effectual to the pardon, if not of sin in a *moral* sense, at least of something analogous to it; and which, by way of distinction, may not improperly be called *legal* sin.

What has now been said is, I trust, sufficient to ascertain the true point upon which

[n] Lev. xiv. 53.
[o] Lev. xiv. 18.
[p] Lev. xv. 15, 30.
[q] Lev. iv. 20, 26, 35.—v. 18.
[r] Lev. vi. 5.
[s] See Serm. III.

the

the controverfy turns. The doctrine of Atonement is, as we have feen, the doctrine of reconciliation; and the queftion, freed from all extraneous and uneffential matter, and reduced to its proper dimenfions, is, whether Chrift immediately by his death propitiated God, and procured for us the benefits of the Gofpel-covenant? The Socinian herefy maintains the negative fide of this queftion, in oppofition to the Catholick Church, which, till thus difturbed, peaceably acquiefced in the affirmative. The Catholic faith, in this important article, I have undertaken to illuftrate and defend: and what I have to offer may fitly be reduced to two general heads, according as its intention is either directly to confirm the doctrine in queftion, or to obviate objections againft it. Agreeably to this divifion, I propofe, in the fequel of thefe Difcourfes,

Firft, to adduce the pofitive proofs which the Scriptures afford in favour of this doctrine: And,

Secondly, to confider the principal objections which its Opponents, and efpecially the Hiftorian of the Corruptions of Chriftianity, have urged againft it.

Upon

SERMON I.

Upon the former of thefe heads I propofe to enter in the next Difcourfe. In the mean time, let no man be difappointed if little fhall be offered to his confideration, with which he was not previoufly acquainted. It would be as difficult as it is unneceffary, to advance any thing new upon a fubject which has been fo often and fo ably difcuffed. In inveftigating any point of Chriftian doctrine, all that can now be expected, and perhaps all that ought to be attempted, is to ftate with accuracy and precifion what the true faith is; and having felected the beft arguments in its defence, to arrange them in the cleareft order, and to place them in the moft ftriking point of view; and if either new objections have been raifed, or old ones revived, to oppofe them with vigour and authority, but with temper and moderation : and whoever performs this fuccefsfully, does no mean fervice to the caufe of truth and religion. Of the prefent attempt it becomes not me to fpeak : I have only to requeft your candid attention to what fhall be offered.

SERMON II.

1 Tim. i. 15.

This is a faithful saying, and worthy of all acceptation, that Christ Jesus came into the world to save sinners.

TO deny that Jesus Christ is the Saviour of mankind, would be in effect to deny the truth of the Gospel, and to renounce the Christian name: and therefore upon this great and fundamental point there can be no question among Christians; all of every sect and denomination must assent to the general doctrine of the text, and, with the Apostle, account it " a faithful saying, and worthy of all " acceptation."

But though Christians must thus in general terms ascribe the salvation of a sinful world to Jesus Christ, yet concerning the method

method of this falvation, and the means by which it was effected, there may prevail, and unhappily there has prevailed, no little difference of opinion. The Hiftorian of the Corruptions of Chriftianity refers it entirely to the *word* and *doctrine* of Chrift: we, in conjunction with the majority of Chriftians, afcribe it immediately to his *death*. According to the former, the Saviour of the world is merely a Prophet, commiffioned to promote by his teaching the reformation of the finner: according to the latter, he is alfo a Prieft, confecrated to appear before God in behalf of mankind, and, by an offering of his own blood, to make reconciliation for fins. In the Socinian fcheme the *death* of the Saviour no otherwife promotes the great end of his miffion, than as it ferves to confirm the doctrine which he taught, and to exhibit a moft perfect example of obedience to God: by the Catholick Church it is accounted the foundation of all our hopes of pardon and acceptance, and the means of procuring for us all the benefits of the Gofpel-covenant. And this faith of the Catholick Church refpecting the prieftly office of our Redeemer, and the efficacy of his death, is that doctrine of Atonement, the proofs of which, agreeably to

SERMON II.

to the plan propofed in my laft Difcourfe, I am now to lay before you.

As *atonement* is a term borrowed from the Levitical law, and, when applied to the work of Chrift for our falvation, is to be taken in its ftrictly legal fenfe, it will much affift our inveftigation of the doctrine in queftion, if, in the firft place, we enquire after what manner the legal atonements were made.

We learn from the Old Teftament, that when the Ifraelites were firft incorporated as a religious body, the Tabernacle was the appointed place of public worfhip; and that for the fervice of the Tabernacle the order of Priefts was inftituted, to whom it exclufively belonged to ftand before God, and to perform, in the name and in behalf of the people, the accuftomed rites of their religion; nor could the members of this facred community, otherwife than through *their* miniftration, make their addreffes to God, or, when excluded from his favour, obtain forgivenefs and reconciliation.

The miniftration of the Priefts confifted for the moft part in offering gifts and facrifices for fin: for the worfhip of the Ifraelites was entirely by facrifice; and all their addreffes to

the

the Deity were performed by means of facrificial rites, which ferved as fymbols or external figns of their internal affections and defires. By facrifice they addreffed themfelves to God either in praife and thankfgiving for paft inftances of his bounty, or in prayer for a continuance of his goodnefs. By facrifice they implored forgivenefs for any fin or uncleannefs, which had feparated them from the congregation of God's people, and had excluded them from the worfhip of the Tabernacle. In this latter cafe (for with thefe facrifices for fin, or fin-offerings as they were commonly called, we are principally concerned) the Prieft interceded for the excluded perfon, by offering or prefenting to God the blood of the appointed victim; by which he was faid to *make atonement:* for the power of making atonement was in the blood, agreeably to the teftimony of God himfelf, when he affigns the reafon of the law which forbids the eating of blood: " For the " life of the flefh is in the blood, and I have " given it to you upon the altar to make an " atonement for your fouls; for it is the blood " that maketh an atonement for the foul [a]."

[a] Lev. xvii. 11.

And

And, in consequence of the atonement thus made, the sinner obtained forgiveness and re-admission to all the privileges of the Covenant.

It appears, then, that under the law two things were generally necessary to atonement; a victim, by the offering of whose blood the atonement was made; and a Priest, by whom the blood was offered. And I conceive that I shall sufficiently prove the doctrine in question, if I can shew from the Scriptures that in the Christian dispensation there are corresponding circumstances; that the death or blood of Christ has a power and influence corresponding to that which in the Old Testament is attributed to the blood of the sin-offerings; and that to Christ himself is ascribed an office and ministry corresponding to that which was formerly discharged by the Levitical Priests in the earthly Tabernacle. In the present Discourse I shall enter upon the proof of the former of these points: viz. that the sacred writers ascribe to the death or blood of Christ a power and influence, corresponding to that which, under the Old Testament, was attributed to the blood of the sin-offerings.

In speaking of the legal atonements[b], I have

[b] Serm. I. p. 28.

already

already had occasion to observe, that the end for which they were appointed, was to recommend and make acceptable to God the things intended for his service, which on account of some uncleanness or pollution were displeasing in his sight: and that, in order to accomplish this end, they had the power of removing both the pollution which had occasioned the Divine displeasure, and also the displeasure itself, to which the pollution had given rise. Accordingly two things are implied in atonement, viz. the purification of the sinner, and the propitiation of the divine Being.

Now by sin we are represented in Scripture as impure, polluted creatures; offensive and displeasing to God, and objects of his wrath and vengeance. But we are also represented as rescued from these evils by the blood of Christ; to which is expressly ascribed the power of cleansing from the pollution of sin, and of procuring for us the favour of a reconciled God.

And in the first place, purification from the pollution of sin is ascribed in the Scriptures to Christ, and to the influence of his blood; by which we are said to be *justified* and *sanctified*. Now to be justified, is to be absolved

from

from guilt, and to be considered as juft and righteous. But St. Paul, fpeaking of Chrift, affures the Romans, that they were "juftified " by his blood ᶜ." Again, to be fanctified, is to be cleanfed from that pollution which renders all mankind, in their natural ftate, odious and offenfive in the fight of God, and to be made holy and fit for his fervice. This fanctifying power the fame Apoftle, in his Epiftle to the Ephefians, gives to the death of Chrift, afferting, that he " loved the Church, and gave " himfelf for it, that he might *fanctify* and " *cleanfe* it ᵈ." And to the fame purpofe, in his Epiftle to Titus, he declares that one of the ends for which Chrift gave himfelf for us, was, that he might " *purify* to himfelf a pe- " culiar people, zealous of good works ᵉ." In the Epiftle to the Hebrews, the blood of Chrift is faid to " *purge* our confcience from " dead works ᶠ;" and we are alfo faid to be " *fanctified* through the offering of the body " of Chrift ᵍ." And St. John, in the moft exprefs language, declares of thofe who walk in the light, *i. e.* who believe the Gofpel, that " the blood of Jefus Chrift *cleanfeth* them

ᶜ Rom. v. 9.   ᵈ Eph. v. 25, 26.   ᵉ Tit. ii. 14.
ᶠ Heb. ix. 14.   ᵍ Heb. x. 10.

"from all sin [h]." And in the Revelation he addresses himself to Christ, under the character of him who " loved us, and *washed* us " from our sins in his own blood [i]."

Secondly, the removal of God's displeasure, and our restoration to his favour, are also ascribed to Christ, who is represented as *appeasing* or *propitiating* God, *making our peace* with him, and *reconciling* us to him. I have already [k] observed, that, in the Levitical law, the Hebrew word כפר, which by our Translators is sometimes rendered *to make atonement for*, and sometimes *to reconcile*, is expressed in the Septuagint version by ἐξιλασκομαι, to appease or make propitious [l]. In conformity to this language, our blessed Lord, in the Epistle to the Hebrews, is called " a merciful and " faithful High Priest, to make reconcilia-" tion (εἰς τὸ ἱλασκεσθαι) for the sins of the " people [m]." And St. John urges it as a proof of the love of God towards us, that he " sent " his Son to be the *propitiation* (ἱλασμον) for " our sins [n]." And in another place he comforts us with the assurance, that, " if we sin, " we have an advocate with the Father, Jesus

[h] 1 John i. 7. [i] Rev. i. 5. [k] Serm. I. p. 14.
[l] Lev. xvi. 16, 17, 20. [m] Heb. ii. 17.
[n] 1 John iv. 10.

" Christ

"Chrift the righteous, who is the *propitia-*
"*tion* (ἱλασμος) for our fins°." And St. Paul,
having afferted that we are juftified freely by
the grace of God, through the redemption
that is in Jefus Chrift, goes on to declare,
that this Jefus " God hath fet forth to be a
"*propitiation* (ἱλαϛηριον) through faith in his
" blood ᵖ."

Many alfo are the paffages which fpeak of
Chrift as our *peace-maker*, and the means of
our *reconciliation* with God: fuch as that of
St. Paul to the Romans, " For if when we
" were enemies we were *reconciled* to God
" by the death of his Son, much more,
" being reconciled, we fhall be faved by his
" life. And not only fo, but we alfo joy
" in God through our Lord Jefus Chrift, by
" whom we have now received the *atone-*
" *ment* ᑫ;" in the original καταλλαγην, *i. e.*
the *reconciliation*, as the word was rendered
in the former part of the paffage ʳ. And
again, in his Epiftle to the Ephefians ; " But
" now in Chrift Jefus, ye, who fometimes
" were far off, are made nigh by the blood
" of Chrift : for he is *our peace*, who hath

° 1 John ii. 2.   ᵖ Rom. iii. 25.
ᑫ Rom. v. 10.   ʳ See Serm. I. p. 14.

" made

"made both one, and hath broken down the
"middle wall of partition between us, hav-
"ing abolished in his flesh the enmity, even
"the law of commandments contained in
"ordinances; for to make in himself of
"twain one new man, so making peace; and
"that he might *reconcile* both unto God in
"one body by the cross, having slain the en-
"mity thereby¹." In this passage the Apostle
makes the death of Christ upon the cross, the
means of letting in the Gentiles to a participation of religious privileges, which before
were confined to the Jews; and by abolish-
ing the ceremonial law, which originally
made, and served still to keep up, a separation
between them, of reducing them both into
one body, and of reconciling both, thus incorporated, to God. And in his Epistle to
the Colossians he affirms, that, having made
peace through the blood of his cross, it pleased
the Father, " by him to *reconcile* all things
" unto himself²."

And thus with respect to those two leading
circumstances, which are necessarily implied
in atonement, and in which, if I may so
speak, the very essence of atonement consists,

¹ Eph. ii. 13, 14, 15, 16.   ² Col. i. 20.

viz.

viz. the purification of the sinner, and the propitiation of the Divine being, the blood of Christ appears to correspond most exactly to that blood which was given upon the Altar under the legal dispensation, and may therefore justly be considered as given for the same end, viz. to make an atonement for the soul.

But besides these positive declarations, ascribing to Christ's blood that same influence by which the legal atonements were effected, there are also in the holy Scriptures various passages, which tend most powerfully to confirm the doctrine in question, by exhibiting the death of Christ under such representations as declare it to be to us, what the sin-offerings were to the Israelites of old, the means of our deliverance from the punishment of sin, and of our restoration to the favour of God.—Of these representations, one of the principal is that of a *price* or *ransom*.

A *price*, in the common acceptation of the word, is something given in exchange for some other thing: and this price becomes a *ransom*, when it is given for the deliverance of a person who is in a state of bondage or captivity; and the deliverance thus obtained is properly called *redemption*. For redemption,

in

in its original and proper meaning, is somewhat more than mere deliverance; it is a *purchased* deliverance—a deliverance effected by the payment of a stipulated price; which price, as above stated, is properly called a *ransom*.

Now the natural state of man is described in Scripture as a state of the most abject and servile bondage. He is said to be sold under sin [u]; to be the servant of sin [w]; to be under the power and dominion of the devil, of whom he is taken captive at his will [x]: and Christ, who delivered us from this bondage, acquired from hence the name of *Redeemer*; the deliverance itself is called our *redemption*; and the *ransom*, or price which he paid for our redemption, is asserted to be his own blood.

In the twenty-fifth chapter of Leviticus, which treats of the redemption of servants, the Septuagint version expresses the act of redeeming by the verb λυτροω; the redemption by λυτρωσις; and the ransom, or price of rededemption, by λυτρον. The same language is used in the New Testament, to express our redemption from the bondage of sin and Satan, and from all the miseries consequent upon

---

[u] Rom. vii. 14.   [w] Rom. vi. 17.   [x] 2 Tim. ii. 26.

the

SERMON II.

the fall, by our Lord and Saviour Jesus Christ. Speaking of himself, he says, that " the Son of Man came to give his life a *ransom* (λυτρον) for many ʸ." And St. Paul says of him, that he " gave himself a *ransom* (αντι- λυτρον) for all ᶻ." And the same Apostle asserts of him, that " in him we have *redemp- tion* (την απολυτρωσιν) through his blood, even the forgiveness of sins ᵃ." And St. Peter says expressly, " ye were not *redeemed* (ελυ- τρωθητε) with corruptible things, as silver and gold,—but with the precious blood of Christ ᵇ."

Of the same import are those passages which represent us simply as having been *bought* or *purchased* by Christ. St. Peter speaks of some " who denied the Lord that *bought* them (τον ἀγορασαντα αυτ*ς*) ᶜ;" and says St. Paul, " ye are *bought* (ηγορασθητε) with a price ᵈ:" which price is expressly speci- fied in the Revelation of St. John, " Thou wast slain, and hast *redeemed* us to God by thy *blood* ᵉ:" the word in the original is ηγορασας, thou hast *purchased* us, or paid for

---

ʸ Matt. xx. 28.   ᶻ 1 Tim. ii. 6.   ᵃ Eph. i. 7. Coll. i. 14.
ᵇ 1 Pet. i. 18, 19.   ᶜ 2 Pet. ii. 1.   ᵈ 1 Cor. vi. 20.
ᵉ Rev. v. 9.

us the price of thy blood. Now that the blood of Chrift, confidered as a price or ranfom, correfponds in power and influence to the fin-offerings under the law, is evident from one of the paffages above quoted, in which the redemption, afcribed to his blood, is exprefsly called *the forgivenefs of fins*; the very benefit which the Ifraelites obtained through the legal atonements.

Another reprefentation of the death of Chrift, much to our prefent purpofe, is that of a *punifhment* undergone for us, and in our ftead.

Under the legal difpenfation, God was pleafed to intimate his acceptance of vicarious fuffering, by the very appointment of victims, the fhedding of whofe blood made atonement for the foul. For fince in this cafe the death of the victim difcharged the finner from all obligation to punifhment, what is this, in reality, but a fubftitution of the former in the room of the latter? And this indeed may be inferred from the very declaration, that it is the *blood that maketh an atonement for the foul:* that is, as the Septuagint renders it, αντι ψυχης, *inftead of* the foul: which implies, that the life of the victim was given and accepted for

the

SERMON II.

the life of the sinner: or, in other words, that the victim was substituted in the room of the sinner. And this is further confirmed by a ceremony, observed at the presentation of a victim, intended for a sin-offering, at the door of the Tabernacle. For he who brought the victim was commanded to lay his hand upon the head of the animal [f]: which action was esteemed an acknowledgment of his own guilt, and a prayer that it might be punished in the victim upon which his hand was laid. And accordingly we find, in the Rabbinical writers, a set form of prayer, which, according to them, was always used upon this occasion. In this form the delinquent acknowledges his offence, and professes his repentance; and concludes with a petition that the victim, upon which he laid his hands, *might be his expiation*. By which last expression he was, as the Jews inform us, understood to mean, that the victim might be substituted in his room, and that the punishment which himself had merited, might fall upon the head of his offering [g].

[f] Lev. iv. 4, 15, 24, 29.
[g] See Outram de Sacrificiis, lib. i. cap. xv. § 10. where the Reader will find the penitential forms which, as the Jews themselves assert, were antiently used on these occasions.

Now

SERMON II.

Now that Chrift was fubftituted in our ftead, may be inferred from the paffages above alleged, which fpeak of his blood as a *price* or *ranfom*. For fince a price is properly that which is given in exchange for fome other thing, it may be confidered as fubftituted in the room of that other; and confequently Chrift, whofe life was given as the price of our deliverance from death, may be confidered as having been fubftituted in our ftead. And to this agree the words of our Lord, above quoted; " The Son of Man came " to give his life a ranfom *for* many;" λυτρον αντι πολλων, a ranfom *inftead of* many: and alfo thofe of St. Paul, " He gave himfelf a " ranfom *for* all;" αντιλυτρον, a ranfom *inftead of* all.

This fubftitution may alfo be inferred from the words of Caiphas the High Prieft, which, as St. John informs us, he fpake prophetically concerning Chrift: " It is," fays he, " expe-
" dient for us that one man fhould die *for*
" the people, and that the whole nation
" perifh not [h]."

And that Chrift was thus fubftituted in our ftead, in order that, by his own fuffering, he

[h] John xi. 50.

might

might deliver us from the punishment due to sin, is manifest from those passages of Scripture which speak of him as *bearing our sins*. Isaiah, prophesying concerning the Messiah, declares, that " the Lord hath *laid on him* " *the iniquity* of us all [1]:" and again, that " he shall *bear the iniquities*," and also that " he *bare the sin* of many [k]." And these prophecies are declared in the New Testament to have been accomplished in the person of our blessed Saviour; who, according to St. Peter, " his own self *bare our sins* in his " own body on the tree [l]." And in the Epistle to the Hebrews it is said that " he " was offered to *bear the sins* of many [m]." Now *to bear sin*, as often as the idea of suffering is implied, is, in Scripture-language, to *bear the punishment of sin*, as is evident from the words of Ezekiel: " The Son shall not " *bear the iniquity* of the Father [n];" where the meaning, undoubtedly, is, the Son shall not be *punished for the iniquity* of the Father.

And that the sufferings of Christ are to be considered in the light of a punishment, is further evident from the words of St. Paul;

[l] Is. liii. 6. [k] Is. liii. 11, 12. [l] 1 Pet. ii. 24.
[m] Heb. ix. 28. [n] Ezek. xviii. 20.

" Christ

SERMON II.

"Chrift hath redeemed us from the curfe of the law, being made a *curfe* for us; for it is written, Curfed is every one that hangeth on a tree[o]." Where by "the curfe of the law" we are to underftand, the punifhment denounced by the law againft fin; from which that we might be delivered, Chrift condefcended to be confidered as a malefactor, and to fuffer as fuch. In the fame fenfe we may alfo underftand the Apoftle in another place; "for he hath made him to be *fin* for us, who knew no fin[p]." To thefe we may add the paffages of Scripture, which affert of Chrift, that he "fuffered for fins the juft for the unjuft[q];" that he "died for the ungodly[r];" that he "gave himfelf for us[s];" that he "died for our fins[t];" and "was delivered for our offences[u]." Thefe, and a variety of fimilar expreffions, which perpetually occur in the Scriptures, all in their plain and obvious fenfe confpire to prove, that Chrift, being fubftituted in our ftead, hath by his fuffering delivered us from that curfe and punifhment, to which, by reafon of fin, we were become obnoxious: in this re-

[o] Gal. iii. 13.   [p] 2 Cor. v. 21.   [q] 1 Pet. iii. 18.
[r] Rom. v. 6.   [s] Tit. ii. 14.   [t] 1 Cor. xv. 3.
[u] Rom. iv. 25.

fpect

spect corresponding to the legal sacrifices for sin, by which a similar deliverance was effected.

I have reserved for the last place those passages of Scripture, in which the death of Christ is represented to us as a sacrifice.

Among the Israelites, the sacrifices, which their law either permitted or prescribed, were of various kinds, and have received different denominations, according to the intention of the worshipper, and the purpose for which they were offered. If the end proposed was to acknowledge a grateful sense of God's goodness, and to return him thanks and praise for past instances of his bounty, the sacrifices employed for this purpose were called *eucharistic*. If God was addressed in order to obtain a continuance of his favour, or to solicit either deliverance from some impending evil, or the grant of some expected good, recourse was had to *vows* and *free-will offerings*. If, again, the worshipper was in a state of sin or uncleanness, and was in consequence separated from the congregation, and excluded from the worship of the Tabernacle, he implored forgiveness and re-admission to his religious privileges, by *expiatory* sacrifices. It is to sacrifices of this latter kind that the writers of the New Testament in general refer, when they speak of Christ as a victim slain and offered for the sins of mankind. Thus when St. Paul, in his Epistle to the Ephesians, asserts of Christ, that he " loved " us, and gave himself for us, an offering and " a sacrifice to God for a sweet-smelling " favour [w]," what is this but ascribing to the death of Christ the same effect which the burnt sacrifices, under the law, once possessed? for from them God is said to have smelled a sweet savour; and they are expressly declared to be " accepted for the offerers, to make " atonement for them [x]."

But the principal sacrifices under the law, to which an expiatory virtue is ascribed, are the *sin-offerings:* and accordingly to them we have most frequent references; and especially to the sin-offerings which were offered on the feast of expiation. Isaiah, who prophesied of the Messiah, that he should bear our iniquities, prophesied also, that his soul should be made an " offering for sin [y];" and, agreeably to this prophecy, we are told, in the Epistle to the Hebrews, that Christ " was " *offered* to bear the sins of many [z];" and that " we are sanctified," that is, delivered from

[w] Eph. v. 2.
[y] Is. liii. x.
[x] Lev. i. 4—9.
[z] Heb. ix. 28.

the

the pollution of sin, " through the *offering* of " his body [a]." It is also with reference to the same sacrifices, that St. Peter, speaking of our redemption by the blood of Christ, calls him " a *lamb* without blemish and without " spot [b]:" and that John the Baptist stiles him " the *lamb* of God which taketh away " the sin of the world [c]." And perhaps the true interpretation of a passage above quoted [d], in which it is said that he was made *sin* for us, is, that he was made a *sin-offering* for us; agreeably to the idiom of the Hebrew language, in which חטאה, which properly signifies *sin*, signifies also the *offering* for sin [e].

But besides these references to the Levitical sacrifices in general, there are other passages of Scripture, which, in speaking of the death of Christ, directly refer to such sacrifices as were appointed to be offered at stated times and upon particular occasions. And this I conceive to be the case with the words delivered by our Lord himself at the institu-

[a] Heb. x. 10.   [b] 1 Pet. i. 19.   [c] John i. 29.
[d] 2 Cor. v. 21.
[e] This idiom is preserved in the Septuagint version, where ἁμαρτια (the very word here used by the Apostle) sometimes signifies *a sin-offering*. See Lev. iv. 21.

SERMON II.

tion of the Eucharift, in which there appears a direct reference to the facrifices offered at the dedication of the Mofaical covenant.

The Eucharift is a facred rite, ordained by our Lord for the exprefs purpofe of continuing in his Church a perpetual memory of his death, and of that peculiar benefit which the fhedding of his blood was to procure for mankind. In this holy facrament bread and wine are the appointed fymbols of his body and blood. Of the bread he fays, " This is my " body :" and of the wine more exprefsly, " This is my blood of the New Teftament, " which is fhed for many, for the remiffion of " fins [f]." The mention of a *New Teftament* naturally reminds us of another, which, by the introduction of this, became *old*, and was ready to vanifh away. And the expreffion, " This is my *blood* of the New Teftament," refers us immediately to that blood which Mofes, when he dedicated the Old Teftament, emphatically calls the *blood of the Covenant*, or *Teftament*, which God had made with his people [g]. The blood of the New Teftament was indeed fhed for *many*; even as many, of whatever nation or kin-

[f] Matt. xxvi. 26, 28.   [g] Exod. xxiv. 8. and Heb. ix. 20.

dred,

dred, as should believe in Jesus; in this respect differing from the blood of the Old Testament, which was shed only for a *single family*, the descendants of Abraham: but the end for which it was shed is the same in both, viz. the remission of sins. That the blood of the Old Testament had in view this end, we affirm upon the authority of the Epistle to the Hebrews: " Whereupon," says the Apostle, " neither the first Testament " was dedicated without blood. For, when " Moses had spoken every precept to all the " people according to the law, he took the " blood of calves and of goats, with water, " and scarlet wool, and hyssop, and sprinkled " both the book and all the people, saying, " This is the blood of the Testament which " God hath enjoined unto you. Moreover, " he sprinkled likewise with blood both the " Tabernacle and all the vessels of the mi- " nistry. And almost all things are by the " law *purged* with blood; and without shed- " ding of blood is no *remission*"." It is evident from this passage, that the sacrifices offered at the dedication of the Old Testament, were of the expiatory kind, and that

ᵇ Heb. ix. 18—22.

the blood then fhed was intended to *purify* the perfons and things included within the covenant; or, as the fame thing is alfo expreffed in other words, to obtain for them *remiffion*; that is, a removal of the guilt or pollution which rendered them unacceptable to God. And the Apoftle immediately proceeds to reafon from the things of the law, which he calls *patterns of things in the heavens*; that is, patterns of the Gofpel-difpenfation, to the Gofpel-difpenfation itfelf; which, he declares, was purified after the fame manner, only with blood of an infinitely higher value. " It was therefore neceffary " that the patterns of things in the heavens " fhould be purified with thefe;" thefe facrifices of brute beafts: " but the heavenly " things themfelves with better facrifices than " thefe [1]," even with the facrifice of Chrift himfelf. Agreeably to our Lord's own declaration, in the paffage more immediately under confideration, where, fpeaking of his own blood, which, in contradiftinction to the blood of the Mofaical covenant, he calls the blood of the New Teftament, he afferts, that it was fhed " for the remiffion of fins." It is

[1] Heb. ix. 23.

therefore

SERMON II.

therefore in the highest degree probable that our Lord, when he instituted the Eucharist, intended a reference to the dedication of the Old Covenant, and to the sacrifices offered upon that occasion. This at least is certain, that, in speaking of his own death, he employs the sacrificial language of the law, and ascribes to his blood that power of cleansing from the pollution of sin, which is attributed, in the Old Testament, to the legal sin-offerings. Consequently the passage before us affords a positive proof that the blood of Christ was intended to make atonement; and was considered in no other light by our Lord himself.

But the most illustrious proof of the point in question may be derived from this same Epistle to the Hebrews, in which the Apostle institutes a comparison, or parallel, between the blood of Christ and that blood which the legal High Priest was accustomed to offer, on the feast of expiation, in the inner Tabernacle, or, as it is commonly called, the Holy of Holies; expressly maintaining, that as, by the sanctifying influence of the latter, the Israelites were qualified for the ceremonial service of the Tabernacle; so by the blood of Christ,

to

to which is afcribed a correfponding influence, Believers are qualified for the fpiritual fervice required by the Gofpel.

But I muft not now enter upon this part of the argument, which will be found fufficiently copious to furnifh matter for a feparate Difcourfe. I fhall therefore referve the full difcuffion of it for the next Lecture.

HEB. ix. 13, 14.

For if the blood of bulls and of goats, and the ashes of an heifer, sprinkling the unclean, sanctifieth to the purifying of the flesh: how much more shall the blood of Christ, who, through the eternal Spirit, offered himself without spot to God, purge your conscience from dead works to serve the living God?

THE design of this Epistle to the Hebrews being to exalt the Christian dispensation, and to assert its pre-eminence above the legal, the Apostle, with this view, among other things, draws a comparison, or parallel, between the blood of Christ and the sin-offerings under the law; attributing to the former a superior efficacy, in accomplishing the very end for which the latter were expressly instituted, viz. the expiation of sin:

thus

thus furnishing us with a most convincing and undeniable argument, in support of the doctrine for which we contend.

The text (in which the above-mentioned parallel is drawn in the strongest and most pointed manner) is naturally divided into two distinct parts or branches. In the former, the Apostle makes mention of certain sacrifices, ordained by the law; to which, in the latter, he opposes the blood of Christ; ascribing to both, though in an unequal degree, a similar power, for the purpose of producing a corresponding effect.

That we may the more readily apprehend the full force of the argument to be derived from this important passage, it will be necessary to enter somewhat at large into the several particulars referred to by the Apostle, and especially those in the first branch of the text; which, accordingly, I shall endeavour to explain in order.

By the " blood of bulls and of goats," the Apostle undoubtedly means those expiatory sacrifices, which were annually offered on a solemn festival, instituted for the express purpose of making an atonement for the whole congregation of the Israelites; and therefore emphatically

phatically called the *feast of expiation*. This is evident from the context, in which mention is made of the High Priest's entrance into the Holy of Holies, with the blood of the sacrifices here referred to; which he was never permitted to do, except upon this occasion. The ceremonies appointed to be used, on each return of this great solemnity, are described at large in the sixteenth chapter of Leviticus. It will be sufficient for our present argument briefly to state, that, after the victims were slain, the High Priest took of the blood, and carried it with him through the vail into the inner Tabernacle, and there offered it, or presented it to God, by sprinkling it with his finger upon and before the mercy-seat; making, by this ceremony, the appointed atonement.

To the blood of bulls and of goats, the Apostle adds, " the ashes of an heifer sprink-" ling the unclean." The law respecting this victim may be found in the nineteenth chapter of the book of Numbers: from which we learn, that a red heifer, in which was no blemish, and upon whose neck the yoke had never come, was brought and slain in presence of the Priest; who took of the blood, and sprinkled it with his finger, seven times,

towards

towards the Tabernacle. The body was then burned before him, and afterwards the afhes were collected, and laid up for the ufe of the congregation, to be applied as occafion required. The mode of application was by taking of the afhes, and pouring upon it running water in a veffel. The unclean perfon was fprinkled with hyffop dipped in this water, and was by this ceremony cleanfed from the pollution which he had contracted.

The text leads us to confider, in the next place, the virtue and efficacy which the blood or afhes of the victims here referred to, was ordained to have; it " fanctified to the pu-
" rifying of the flefh." It fanctified—in the original ἁγιαζει, a word frequently ufed, in the Septuagint verfion, to fignify fuch a cleanfing or purification of a thing taken from common ufe, as confecrates it, or makes it holy and meet for the fervice of God [a]. The Ifraelites were a people precifely in this fituation. God had felected them from the reft of mankind, had called them with a holy calling, and prepared them for his own immediate fervice. As his peculiar people, they enjoyed advan-

[a] See below, p. 74

tages

tages and privileges, to which the other nations of the earth had no pretenſion; eſpecially the glorious privilege of acceſs to God, whoſe viſible preſence diſplayed in the Tabernacle they were permitted to approach. While other nations were afar off, and, as it were, without God in the world, cut off from all communion with him, and even unacquainted with his name, They were the favoured people of the Moſt High, who condeſcended to make a covenant with them, and to dwell among them. While other nations were left to the ſuggeſtions of their own corrupt imaginations, without the knowledge of their duty, and without encouragement to practiſe it, They had a guide to inſtruct, and promiſes to allure them: God gave to them a written law for the direction of their conduct, and covenanted to accept and reward that worſhip and ſervice which himſelf had enjoined. Separate from the reſt of mankind, and forbidden to participate in their wicked and abominable practices, they were deemed a holy people, called to a holy ſervice, and made capable of performing it with acceptance.

It was to give them this capacity (in which conſiſted their diſtinguiſhing character), that

that they were originally *sanctified*, in the sense above assigned to the word ἁγιάζει, here used by the Apostle. For nothing common or unclean can be acceptable to a pure and holy God; nor is any one qualified to be employed in his service, who does not possess such a purity and holiness as is suited to the nature of the service to which he is called. And since the Israelites, before their call, were not exempt from that pollution, which renders all mankind, in their natural state, unfit for communion with God, it pleased him to remove this unfitness, and, by a purification of the uncleanness which occasioned it, to prepare the chosen race for that holy service to which they were appointed. And for this purpose he ordained certain sacrifices, to the blood of which he annexed a cleansing and sanctifying influence; for, as the Apostle, speaking of this very subject, testifies, in the chapter before us, " almost all things are by " the law purged with blood [b]," purged from the uncleanness which naturally adheres to them, and made holy and meet for the service of God. Hence, at the original dedication of the covenant, Moses sprinkled all the

[b] Heb. ix. 22.

people with the blood of the facrifices offered upon that occafion[c]. By this ceremony they were purified, and incorporated as a religious body, and were made capable of approaching the prefence of God, and of performing to him an acceptable fervice.

But the privilege, thus conferred, was not to continue for ever. It pleafed God to make with his people only a temporary covenant, which he ordained fhould be renewed from year to year continually. And for this purpofe he inftituted a folemn feftival, called the Day of Expiation; on every return of which he commanded that the whole congregation, with every thing appertaining to religious worfhip, fhould be purified, and, as it were, dedicated anew, by a re-confecration. And fince individuals among the people were liable to contract occafional impurities, fufficient to exclude them from the Divine prefence, provifion was made for the purification of fuch excluded members, in order that they might be re-admitted to their religious privileges. The facrifices referred to by the Apoftle in the text, were exprefsly inftituted for each of thefe occafions. There is afcribed

[c] Exod. xxiv. 8.

to them a sanctifying power; a power of cleansing from pollution, and of making meet for God's service. By " the blood of bulls and " of goats" the whole congregation, on the appointed festival, was cleansed and sanctified, and the covenant renewed and confirmed : the " ashes of an heifer sprinkling the unclean," removed occasional impurities, and restored the worshipper to those religious privileges, from which his uncleanness had excluded him.

The nature of the pollution, for which a remedy was thus provided by the law, is sufficiently declared by the Apostle, when he affirms, that the rites in question " sanctified to " the *purifying of the flesh :*" from which we may understand, that, under the old covenant, mere *external* uncleanness, which affected only the body of the worshipper, was sufficient to exclude him from the service of God, and must be removed before he could be restored to his religious privileges. This is evident from the law itself, which frequently, and indeed commonly, ordains purification, in cases where there is either no possibility of *moral* uncleanness, or no ground to impute it. Inanimate things are, undoubtedly, incapable

of

of moral uncleanness; yet these, as many of them as were appointed to any sacred office, were commanded to be cleansed and sanctified. Thus, at the dedication of the covenant, Moses sprinkled with blood not only the people, but also " the Tabernacle, and all " the vessels of the ministry [d]." And at the consecration of Aaron and his family to the service of the Tabernacle, their *garments* were sanctified no less than their persons. " And thou shalt take of the blood that is " upon the altar, and of the anointing oil, " and sprinkle it upon Aaron and upon his " garments, and upon his sons, and upon the " garments of his sons with him: and he " shall be hallowed (in the Greek ἁγιασθη- " σεται), and his garments, and his sons, and " his sons' garments with him [e]." And soon after, when Moses is directed to consecrate the *Altar*, the command to him is, " And " thou shalt offer every day a bullock for a " sin-offering for atonement, and thou shalt " *cleanse* the Altar when thou hast made an " atonement for it (εν τω ἁγιαζειν σε επ' αυτω). " And thou shalt anoint it, to sanctify it (ὡςε " ἁγιασαι αυτο) [f]."

[d] Heb. ix. 21.   [e] Exod. xxix. 21.
[f] Exod. xxix. 36.

And as the law thus ordains purification in cafes where there is no capacity of moral uncleannefs, fo likewife cafes may be adduced, in which, whatever the capacity may be, there is, neverthelefs, no ground to impute it. The *leprofy*, for example, is a difeafe which no man willingly brings upon himfelf, and for which no man is juftly chargeable with blame: and yet the leper was accounted unholy, and unfit to appear before God; and was accordingly feparated from the congregation, and excluded from the worfhip of the Tabernacle. The fame was alfo the effect of involuntary difcharges of blood, and other impurities [g]. And in each of thefe cafes the law provided certain facrifices and ceremonies, by which the difeafed perfon, even after he was healed of his plague, was required to be cleanfed, before he was permitted to appear before God in the affembly of his people [h].

The rites, with which our prefent fubject is more immediately concerned, will be found, upon examination, to have no greater virtue or efficacy than thofe already mentioned. As to the burnt heifer, the matter

[g] Lev. xiii. 45, 46. Num. v. 2.   [h] Lev. xiv. 4.—xv. 31.

will not admit of dispute: for by referring to the law respecting this victim, we shall find that its ashes were never applied but for the purification of *external* uncleanness. If any man touched the body of one who had died a natural death [i], or even came into the tent where a dead body was lying [k]; or if he touched the body of one who had been slain with a sword in the open fields; or if he touched the bone of a man, or a grave [l]; in all these cases he was accounted unclean, and was purified by being sprinkled, in the manner above described, with the ashes of the burnt heifer [m]. And not only the man who touched the dead body, was unclean, but the tent also in which the dead body lay, and all the vessels, and every thing that was in the tent, were all unclean, and were purified by the same ceremony [n].

It is evident, then, from the express language of the law itself respecting one of the victims here mentioned by the Apostle, that it was intended solely for the purification of external uncleanness. With respect to the sacrifices offered on the feast of expiation, it

[i] Num. xix. 11. [k] Num. xix. 14. [l] Num. xix. 16. [m] Num. xix. 17. [n] Num. xix. 18.

may be thought, perhaps, at firſt view, that the law aſcribes to them a much higher power: for we read that this ſolemn feſtival was inſtituted " to make an atonement for the " children of Iſrael for *all* their ſins [o]." And among the ceremonies obſerved on this occaſion, the High Prieſt was commanded to confeſs, over the ſcape goat, " *all* the iniquities of " the children of Iſrael, and *all* their tranſgreſ- " ſions in *all* their ſins [p] ;" which ſtrong expreſſions, added to the ſolemnity of the whole proceeding, ſeem to intimate, that the end propoſed by theſe ſacrifices, was the expiation of ſomewhat more than mere external uncleanneſs. But this was not the caſe. For the virtue of this atonement was not confined to the perſons of the Iſraelites, but was extended alſo to the Tabernacle, and to all the things employed in the ſervice of God. For when the High Prieſt ſprinkled the blood upon the mercy-ſeat, and before the mercy-ſeat, we read that the intention of this ceremony was to *make an atonement for the holy place* [q]. And again, when having finiſhed the ceremonies within the Tabernacle, he is commanded to go out unto the altar of burnt-offering, which

[o] Lev. xvi. 34. [p] Lev. xvi. 21. [q] Lev. xvi. 16.

ſtood

stood at the door of the Tabernacle, to sprinkle it also with blood, it is for the express purpose of *making an atonement for it* [r]. And when the prescribed ceremonies are all ended, he is expressly said to have " made an " end of reconciling the holy place, and the " Tabernacle of the congregation, and the " Altar [s]." But since the Tabernacle, and the vessels employed in the service of the Tabernacle, were none of them capable of *moral* guilt, but nevertheless needed expiation, whence the necessity of this expiation, unless to purify them from that *external* uncleanness which naturally adheres to all terrestrial things? And since it is no where said that the atonement made for the holy place differed, either in kind, or in the reasons of its establishment, from that which was made for the worshippers, does it not follow that the pollution was in both the same, and, consequently, that the end proposed by these sacrifices, was no other than the expiation of mere *external* uncleanness?

Nor let it be any objection, that the impurities, for which this expiation was provided, are expressly called *iniquities* and *sins*. For

[r] Lev. xvi. 18.   [s] Lev. xvi. 20.

these terms do not, in the language of the Old Testament, necessarily imply a deviation from *moral* rectitude, or a transgression of the *moral* law; but are frequently used, when nothing more can be understood than a privation of that bodily purity which the *ceremonial* law required. Thus we read of the *iniquity of the sanctuary*, which, it is said, the Priests shall bear [t]. And Aaron is commanded to wear, as a fore-front to the mitre, upon his forehead a plate of gold, on which was engraven, HOLINESS TO THE LORD, that he " may bear the *iniquity of the holy things,* " which the children of Israel shall hallow in " all their holy gifts [u]." Thus also the ashes of the burnt heifer, though applied only for the purification of external uncleanness, is nevertheless expressly called " the ashes of the " burnt heifer of purification for *sin* [w]." And again, when a man recovered from a leprosy, or other involuntary disease, which the law accounted unclean, he was required to offer for his cleansing a *sin*-offering [x]. Thus, free from blame as the unclean person must be esteemed in a moral point of view, in the eye

[t] Numb. xviii. 1.
[w] Num. xix. 17.
[u] Exod. xxviii. 38.
[x] Lev. xiv. 19.

of the law he was not guiltless: he was deemed a sinner; and one whose sin was of so polluting a nature, as to defile even the Tabernacle of the Most High. And he, who, being in a state of legal uncleanness, still presumed, regardless of the Divine ordinances, to join the congregation of God's people, and to approach the Divine presence, was accounted worthy of no less a punishment than death. " The man," says the law respecting the burnt heifer, " that shall be unclean, " and shall not purify himself, that soul shall " be cut off from the congregation: because " he hath defiled the Tabernacle of the " Lord; the water of separation hath not " been sprinkled upon him; he *is* un- " clean ʸ."

And this power of the Levitical sacrifices to expiate only legal sins, is what the Apostle must be understood to mean, not only in the text, but also at the ninth verse of this chapter, where he virtually denies that they have any higher power; positively asserting, that " they could not make him that did the ser- " vice, perfect, as pertaining to the con- " science: μη δυναμεναι κατα συνειδησιν τελειωσαι

ʸ Num. xix. 20.

τον

τον λατρευοντα"—of which paſſage, if we give to the word τελειωσαι the ſenſe which, when uſed on ſimilar occaſions, it bears in the Septuagint verſion [z], the meaning will be, " They could " not *conſecrate* the worſhipper, or qualify him " for the office of ſerving God, by purifying " the conſcience." God had given to them no ſuch power; nor were they in their own nature fitted for ſuch a work; inaſmuch as they conſiſted ſolely in external obſervances, and in rites with which the body, and not the conſcience, of the worſhipper, was concerned: or, to uſe the Apoſtle's own language, " they ſtood only in meats and drinks, " and divers waſhings, and *carnal* ordinances, " impoſed on them until the time of reform-" ation [a];" until he who was the end of the law ſhould come, and be the Mediator of a better covenant, eſtabliſhed upon better promiſes than was this of Moſes.

[z] In the twenty-ninth chapter of Exodus, which preſcribes the ceremonies to be obſerved in the conſecration of Aaron and his ſons to the Prieſt's office, this word frequently occurs in the ſenſe here aſſigned to it; and in this Epiſtle to the Hebrews, it is alſo once taken by our Tranſlators in the ſame ſenſe. " For the law maketh men High " Prieſts which have infirmity: but the word of the oath, " which was ſince the law, maketh the Son, who is *conſe-*" *crated* (τετελειωμενον) for evermore." ch. vii. 28.
[a] Heb. ix. 10.

It

It appears, then, as well from the law itself, as from the declaration of the Apostle, that the rites and sacrifices to which the text refers, were intended solely to cleanse the body of the worshipper from those impurities which, under the legal economy, disqualified him from performing to God an acceptable service; they " sanctified to the purifying of the flesh." The Apostle next asserts the superior efficacy of Christ's blood, to qualify for the service of God under the Christian dispensation. If the blood of the Levitical sacrifices, carried by the High Priest into the Holy of Holies, had the power here ascribed to it, of purifying the bodies of the Israelites, rendering them holy and meet for the service to which they were called, " how much " more shall the blood of Christ, who through " the eternal spirit offered himself without " spot to God, purge your conscience from " dead works, to serve the living God ?"

It is evident at first view, that *the blood of Christ*, in this latter part of the text, is made to correspond with *the blood of bulls and of goats*, mentioned in the former part. For these two are directly opposed to each other. " If the blood of bulls and of
" goats"

"goats"—"how much more the blood of "Chrift?" And as on the feaft of expiation the blood of the former was offered by the High Prieft, who for that purpofe entered with it through the vail into the inner Tabernacle, fo Chrift is faid to have entered into heaven itfelf *with his own blood*[b], and, as the text exprefsly afferts, to have " offered " *himfelf* to God." And this offering is further faid to poffefs the general qualification required in all the legal offerings (and in thofe appointed for the feaft of expiation among the reft), concerning which the law ordains, that they fhould be perfect in their kind, and without blemifh[c]: for Chrift " offered himfelf *without fpot* to God." The fpotlefs purity required in the legal victims as to their bodies, he poffeffed inwardly in his foul; " he did no fin, neither was guile " found in his mouth[d];" and is therefore not unaptly ftiled by St. Peter a *lamb*, the emblem of purity and innocence; " a lamb " without blemifh and without fpot[e]."

It is alfo evident, that *internal* pollution, or thofe defilements of the confcience which

[b] Heb. ix. 12, 24. [c] Lev. xxii. 20, 21.
[d] 1 Pet. ii. 22. [e] 1 Pet. i. 19.

arise from sin in a *moral* sense, is here made to correspond with *external* pollution, or those bodily defilements which were occasioned by *legal* sin. And as the blood of the legal offerings had the power of cleansing the polluted *bodies* of the Israelites, and of purifying them from that uncleanness which excluded them from the Divine presence, so even in a greater degree (for the Apostle here argues from the less to the greater) has the blood of Christ the power of cleansing the polluted *consciences* of Believers, and of purifying them from the stain of those evil works, the wages, or natural desert of which, is death [f], or total exclusion, and everlasting destruction, from the presence of the Lord. " How much " more shall the blood of Christ purge your " *conscience* from dead works ?"

It is further evident, that the *spiritual* worship and service of the Gospel is here made to correspond with the *carnal* ordinances, and outward observances of the law. And as the blood of the legal offerings sanctified the Israelites, and qualified them for the ceremonial worship of the Tabernacle, so the blood of Christ sanctifies the Christian Church, and qualifies the true Believer for communion

[f] Rom. vi. 23.

with

with God, and for performing with acceptance that pure and spiritual service which is required of him. " How much more shall " the blood of Chrift purge your confcience " from dead works, *to ferve the living God?*"

And thus does the blood of Chrift correspond, in all effential points, to the Levitical facrifices for fin. It is exprefsly called an offering; is affirmed, like the legal offerings, to be perfect and without fpot; and, like them alfo, to have the power of cleanfing from pollution, and of qualifying for the fervice of God. In point of real worth and excellence, the legal offerings fell indeed infinitely fhort of the offering made by Chrift. For the blood which was carried by the High Prieft within the vail, though accepted by God, was after all but the blood of brute beafts, and therefore in itfelf of very little worth. Whereas Chrift made, in the heavenly Sanctuary, an offering of his own blood, even the blood of the Son of God; an offering than which the whole extent of nature could not furnifh one more valuable in itfelf, or more precious in the fight of God, of whofe acceptance it was every way worthy.

And as the evangelical offering is thus more

more valuable and excellent, fo is its efficacy proportionably greater and more extenfive. The legal offerings could only cleanfe the bodies of the Ifraelites, polluted with legal fin: but the blood of Chrift extends its cleanfing influence even to the foul: it purges the confcience from dead works; from works for which the law was fo far from providing an atonement, that it annexed to them the penalty of death: and confecrates the finner to a pure and fpiritual fervice; a fervice as far exceeding the ceremonial fervice of the Tabernacle, as the inward purity of heart and mind, required by the Gofpel, exceeds the mere outward cleanlinefs of the body, which the law prefcribes; and therefore more worthy in itfelf, and, when performed in fincerity, more acceptable to God, than the moft rigid and exact compliance with all the precepts of the Jewifh ritual.

The text, thus explained, applies moft readily to the doctrine for which we are contending, and affords, if I miftake not, an incontrovertible argument in its fupport. This argument I know not how to fet in a ftronger point of view, than by a brief recapitulation of what has been offered.

We

SERMON III.

We learn from the law, given to the defcendants of Abraham, that by fin, in a *legal* fenfe, as it fignifies that outward impurity which affects the body, the Ifraelites were accounted unclean, and unfit to appear before God in the affembly of his people. And we learn from the law of nature, no lefs than from the revealed will of God, that by fin in a *moral* fenfe, as it fignifies that inward corruption of heart and life which affects the confcience, we are all unclean, and unfit for any communion with him, who is of purer eyes than to behold iniquity. For the former of thefe fins the law provided a remedy, by appointing facrifices, to the blood or afhes of which was annexed the power of purifying the flefh, and of reftoring the unclean perfon to thofe religious privileges, from which his uncleannefs had excluded him. The fame, and even greater efficacy is by the Apoftle afcribed to the blood of Chrift, in purifying the confcience; in cleanfing thofe who are defiled with moral guilt, and in removing that inability which cut them off from communion with God, and rendered them unfit for his fervice. " If," fays the Apoftle, " the blood of bulls and of goats, " and the afhes of an heifer, fprinkling the
" unclean,

SERMON III.

" unclean, sanctifieth to the purifying of the flesh; how much more shall the blood of Christ, who through the eternal Spirit offered himself without spot to God, purge your conscience from dead works to serve the living God?" Now since *atonement* was the acknowledged consequence of that cleansing influence which is here ascribed to these Levitical sacrifices for sin, who, after the parallel thus drawn by the Apostle, is prepared to assert, that the offering, which Christ is said to have made of himself to God, was not for atonement also?

Having now, in this and the preceding Discourse, laid before you what appears to me the most material part of that abundant evidence which the Scriptures afford, in support of the first position which I undertook to prove, it may be of use in this place briefly to observe, by way of recapitulation, that the proofs of this position have been derived, first, from the positive declarations of Scripture, which ascribe to the blood of Christ the general effects and properties of a *propitiatory* sacrifice: secondly, from the scriptural representations of his death, by which

which it is exhibited to us under the three following views—as a price, as a puniſhment, and as a ſin-offering: thirdly, and chiefly, from that expreſs compariſon, with reſpect to this very point, which the Apoſtle to the Hebrews inſtitutes between the Law and the Goſpel. And from the whole it is, I truſt, ſufficiently manifeſt, that the ſacred writers aſcribe to the blood or death of Chriſt a power and influence, correſponding to that which, under the Old Teſtament, was attributed to the ſacrifices for ſin.

The next thing to be ſhewn, is, that the Scriptures aſcribe to Chriſt himſelf an office and miniſtry, correſponding to that which was antiently diſcharged by the Levitical Prieſts in the Tabernacle erected by Moſes. And this I ſhall make the ſubject of the next Diſcourſe.

SERMON

SERMON IV.

HEB. viii. 1, 2.

We have such an High Priest, who is set on the right hand of the throne of the Majesty in the heavens; a minister of the Sanctuary, and of the true Tabernacle which the Lord pitched, and not man.

THE connection of the Law with the Gospel, and the end for which, considered as so connected, it was originally ordained, is virtually asserted by St Paul, in his Epistle to the Galatians. " The law," says he, " was our schoolmaster, to bring us unto " Christ [a]." By which we may understand that the legal dispensation was instituted for the times before the coming of our Lord, to

[a] Gal. iii. 24.

prepare the people of God for the appearance of the promised Saviour, and to instruct them in the nature and design of his mission. This was its original end and designation: and in order to accomplish this end, it was so disposed by Divine wisdom, as to correspond, in all essential points, to that better dispensation, by which in the fulness of time it was to be succeeded, and of which it is expressly called the *type*, that is, the *pattern* or *model*.

Nor is the benefit yet ceased. For now, that this better dispensation is fully established, it no less serves for our instruction in the knowledge of Christ and his religion: and we may promise to ourselves no little assistance in elucidating any obscure or disputed point relating to the Gospel, by referring it (under the direction of the holy Scriptures) to its corresponding circumstance in the law. Of its use in this respect we have already had abundant experience: let us therefore, in the succeeding part of our enquiry, pursue the same method: and as we before shewed that the blood of Christ has a power and efficacy, corresponding to that which is attributed to the sacrifices for sin under the Old Testament; so let us now enquire, whether the Scriptures do not ascribe to Christ himself an office and ministry,

ministry, corresponding to that which was antiently discharged by the Levitical Priests in the Tabernacle erected by Moses.

Under the legal œconomy the priesthood was confined to the family of Aaron, which was taken from among the children of Israel, and appointed to stand before God in the holy place, and to minister unto him. The nature and design of their office may be learned from the Epistle to the Hebrews. " Every " High Priest," says the Apostle, " taken " from among men, is ordained for men in " things pertaining to God, that he may " offer both gifts and sacrifices for sins [b]." He is indeed, as we presently after read, " called " of God [c]," deriving all his title, to perform the functions of his office, from Divine appointment: but " he is ordained for men," acting on their behalf, and for their benefit, " in things pertaining to God;" performing the accustomed rites of religion, in order that he may propitiate God, and make reconciliation for sins. Now what the Apostle here asserts of the High Priest, of whom his subject led him particularly to speak, is equally

[b] Heb. v. 1.   [c] Heb. v. 4.

true

true of all the Priests. They were all "called of "God," and were all appointed to "offer gifts "and sacrifices for sins:" it may therefore be said of them all, that they were "ordained for "men in things pertaining to God." And hence we infer in general, that the priesthood was instituted for the benefit of *men*, but that the Priest, in the execution of his office, had respect unto *God*, to whom his ministry was immediately addressed. A Priest, therefore, may be considered as the Mediator between God and men, or, as the Advocate of men with God, commending them and their concerns to the Divine favour and protection, and interceding for them, that, notwithstanding their sins and offences, God would not for ever cast them out of his favour, but would at length cease from his displeasure, and again be gracious unto them.

That interposition may in any case be attended with success, two qualifications are especially required in a Mediator: first, that he be acceptable to the person with whom he interposes; for without an interest of this kind, the interposition would be impertinent and presumptuous, and consequently unsuccessful: secondly, that he be seriously concerned for the welfare of those for whom he

interposes;

interpofes; otherwife, whatever his intereft might be, it would be weakly and ineffectually exerted. In both thefe refpects the legal Priefts were duly qualified to interpofe between God and his people. They were a holy race, called by God himfelf, and feparated to their holy function by folemn rites of confecration: they were purified by ablutions and facrifices, were fprinkled with the confecrating oil, and invefted with hallowed garments; and were thus fitted and prepared to perform with acceptance that holy fervice to which they were called. And as the fanctity, thus impreffed upon their character, rendered them acceptable Mediators to God, fo their relation to the people, from among whom they were taken, engaged them to a faithful and earneft difcharge of their miniftry. They were all, both Priefts and People, defcended from one common ftock, and were all included within the fame covenant: and therefore the Prieft had a real intereft in the welfare of the People; and being, moreover, himfelf encompaffed with infirmity, he was taught to pity and relieve the infirmities of his brethren.

The interceffion of the Prieft is neceffarily implied in his offering for fin: and whoever

SERMON IV.

among the Israelites, on account of any sin or uncleanness, was excluded from the worship of the Tabernacle, could only recover the Divine favour through the intercession of the Priest, who was said on these occasions *to make atonement*; which he ordinarily did by appearing before God in the holy place, with the blood of the appointed victim. An offering of blood was not indeed so absolutely required, but that on particular occasions the law in this respect was relaxed; as in the case of extreme poverty, when the substitution of a less expensive offering was allowed [d]. But on all occasions the ministry of the Priest was so indispensably necessary, that without it no atonement could be made. Hence atonement is usually ascribed to the act of the Priest; and if any man had committed any sin, or had contracted any uncleanness, for which the law had provided an atonement, he was commanded to take the appointed offering to the Priest; and " the Priest," says the law, " shall make an atonement for him, " for his sin which he hath sinned, and it shall " be forgiven him [e];" and again, in the case of an unclean person, " and the Priest shall

[d] Lev. v. 11.   [e] Lev. v. 10, 13.

" make

SERMON IV. 89

"make an atonement for him, and he shall
"be clean [f]." So again on the feast of expiation, when an atonement was annually made for the Tabernacle, the Altar, and the whole Congregation, it was only by the ministry of the High Priest, that the sanctifying power which the blood possessed, was applied, and, as it were, called forth into action [g]. And thus, as on the one hand the Priest could not ordinarily make atonement without an offering of blood; so neither, on the other, was the blood effectual, unless offered by the Priest: to his act the atonement is expressly ascribed; and only by his intercession was forgiveness to be obtained.

In like manner, under the Gospel-dispensation, forgiveness of sins, and our reconciliation to God, are ascribed to the intercession of Jesus Christ. He is expressly called our "Advocate "with the Father [h];" "a High Priest over "the house of God [i];" "a minister of the" heavenly "sanctuary, and of the true Taber- "nacle, which the Lord pitched, and not man." And this ministry he is said to have obtained,

[f] Lev. xiv. 20.   [g] Lev. xvi. 16, 33.
[h] 1 John ii. 1.   [i] Heb. x. 21.

like

like the legal Priests, by the exprefs appointment of God himfelf: for as under the law, "no man taketh this honour unto himfelf, "but he that is called of God, as was Aaron; "fo alfo, Chrift glorified not himfelf, to be "made an High Prieft; but he that faid "unto him, Thou art my fon, to-day have I "begotten thee [k]."

The qualifications, neceffary to enfure fuccefs to the interpofition of a mediator, are alfo afcribed to Chrift. He is both acceptable to God, and compaffionately affected towards men. The legal Priefts derived their acceptablenefs from the fanctity of their character. In like manner the Apoftle affirms, "that "fuch an High Prieft became us, who is "holy, harmlefs, undefiled, feparate from "finners [l]." And, when fpoken of in the character of our advocate with the Father, he is exprefsly called "Jefus Chrift *the righteous* [n]." And by this fpotlefs purity, this holinefs of foul and fpirit, typified by the external fanctity of the legal Priefts, he is eminently qualified to appear before God: and we are further affured, that his mediation is, in a peculiar manner, acceptable to his heavenly Fa-

[k] Heb. v. 4, 5.   [l] Heb. vii. 26.   [m] 1 John ii. 1.

ther, who declared of him by a voice from heaven, " This is my beloved Son, in whom " I am well pleased [n]." To this acceptableness in the sight of God, the Apostle adds a compassionate regard for men, which he derived from having himself experienced the infirmities of our nature. " For we have not " an High Priest which cannot be touched " with the feeling of our infirmities; but was " in all points tempted like as we are, yet " without sin [o]." " For verily he took not on " him the nature of angels, but he took on " him the seed of Abraham: wherefore in " all things it behoved him to be made like " unto his brethren; that he might be a " merciful and faithful High Priest in things " pertaining to God, to make reconciliation " for the sins of the people. For in that he " himself hath suffered, being tempted, he is " able to succour them that are tempted [p]."

And not only do the sacred writers ascribe to Christ the title and qualifications requisite for the priesthood, but also the peculiar functions of the office; declaring, that in the heavenly sanctuary he made an offering to God, even an offering of himself, or of his

[n] Matt. iii. 17.   [o] Heb. iv. 15.   [p] Heb. ii. 16, 17, 18.

SERMON IV.

own blood [q]: that he put away sin by the sacrifice of himself [r]: that he by himself purged our sins [s]: that he sanctified the people with his own blood [t]: that he appears for us in the presence of God [u]: that he is at the right hand of God, making intercession for us [w]: all of them acts purely sacerdotal, and which cannot be ascribed to Christ in any but the priestly character.

But the truth of our general position will more fully appear, by attending to the parallel which the Apostle, in his Epistle to the Hebrews, draws between the Law and the Gospel. For this parallel is not confined to the corresponding circumstances, with respect to which it has been already considered; viz. the blood of Christ, and that of the legal sacrifices offered by the High Priest on the feast of expiation; but is extended also to Christ and the High Priest considered personally, between whom a correspondence, no less exact, is expressly maintained.

Of all the Priests who officiated in the Tabernacle, the High Priest, as his name

[q] Heb. ix. 12, 14.
[s] Heb. i. 3.
[u] Heb. ix. 24.
[r] Heb. ix. 26.
[t] Heb. xiii. 12.
[w] Rom. viii. 34.

imports,

imports, was the chief. He was selected from among the first-born, and was initiated by the solemn ceremony of anointing. To his character and office a peculiar holiness was annexed; and to his administration was committed that most sacred rite, by which the covenant was annually renewed and confirmed: for to him it exclusively belonged to offer for sin on the feast of expiation; and thus, while the ministry of the inferior Priests was confined to the sanctuary, or outer Tabernacle, he was permitted to enter within the vail into the Holy of Holies, or inner Tabernacle: and his ministry in this most holy place is expressly said to prefigure the ministry of Christ in the heavenly sanctuary, that " true tabernacle, which the Lord pitched, " and not man."

Under the legal economy there was a double oblation of the victims intended for atonement. Of these the first took place while the victim was yet alive; and was made by the presentation of the animal itself at the door of the Tabernacle. But by this oblation no atonement was made: it was preparatory merely to that second and grand oblation, which took place within the Tabernacle, after the blood of the victim was shed.

On

SERMON IV.

On the feast of expiation, the first oblation was made by the High Priest, who presented the victims, selected for this occasion, before the Lord at the door of the Tabernacle, setting them apart by this ceremony, and *sanctifying*, or consecrating them to that holy service for which they were appointed. Corresponding to this oblation was our Saviour Christ's voluntary resignation of himself to that painful and ignominious death which he suffered for our sake; in reference to which he says of himself, in that prayer of his recorded by St. John, which he addressed to God immediately before his passion, that he *sanctified himself* for his Disciples[x]: that is, as Commentators observe, that he offered himself to God as a piacular victim[y]. Agreeably to which St Paul asserts, that he "became obedient "unto death, even the death of the cross[z]:" and in another place more expressly, he "gave "himself for us, an offering and a sacrifice to "God[a]."

The second oblation (with which we are principally concerned in the present argument) was made in the inner Tabernacle,

[x] John xvii. 19. [y] Vid. Whitby in loc.
[z] Phil. ii. 8. [a] Eph. v. 2.

into

SERMON IV.

into which the High Priest, on this feast of expiation, and never on any other occasion, entered alone through the vail with the blood of the appointed sacrifices; which he there offered, by sprinkling it with his finger, upon and before the mercy-seat [b]. The inner Tabernacle was the place in which God was said to dwell; for there his glory was visibly displayed, from between the two cherubims which overshadowed the mercy-seat [c]; and is therefore an apt representation of heaven, the brightest habitation of God's holiness and glory, into which Christ, as the Apostle assures us, is now entered with his own blood; and that for the express purpose, as the Apostle further assures us, of offering it to God [d].

But not only does the Apostle assign to Christ, for the discharge of his ministry, a place corresponding to that of which the High Priest was exclusively the minister; he further ascribes to the ministry of each, in his respective place, a corresponding effect.

In speaking of the feast of expiation, I have already, in a former discourse [e], had oc-

---

[b] Lev. xvi. 14, 15. [c] Exod. xxv. 8, 22. Pf. lxxx. 1.
[d] Heb. ix. 12, 14. [e] Serm. III.

casion to consider the reasons of its establishment, and the efficacy of that blood, which the High Priest was accustomed to offer in the Holy of Holies. It will therefore be sufficient in this place briefly to observe, that, at the original dedication of the covenant, when the Israelites were first incorporated as a religious body, it pleased God to consecrate them, and separate them to his service, by ordaining, that they, and every thing to be employed in religious worship, should be purged with blood. And, as he was pleased to make with them only a temporary covenant, he further thought fit to ordain an annual repetition of this ceremonial of consecration: and for this purpose he instituted the feast of expiation; on every return of which he commanded that the whole congregation, with every thing appertaining to religious worship, should be purified, and, as it were, consecrated anew: which was accordingly done, by the offering of the High Priest in the Holy of Holies. From all which it appears, that the effect, produced by the ministry of the High Priest, was nothing less than the consecration of the whole legal economy for the ensuing year; the purification of the Tabernacle, that it might be a fit residence for the Deity; and the

the sanctification of the people, that they might be qualified for the holy service to which they were called.

In like manner the Christian Church was sanctified and prepared, by the offering of the blood of Christ. " It was necessary," says the Apostle, " that *the patterns of things in the heavens* should be purified with these" sacrifices of beasts, " but the *heavenly things themselves* with better sacrifices than these[f];" even with the sacrifice of Christ himself. And again, speaking of the offering which Christ made of himself in heaven, he declares, that by this offering he " *perfected* them that are " sanctified [g];" he perfected; in the original τετελειωκεν, he *consecrated* or *dedicated*; for such, as I have already observed [h], is the meaning of the word, when used on similar occasions, in the Septuagint version: and that it can have no other meaning in this passage, is evident from the whole scope of the Apostle's argument, which manifestly requires that the same effect should be ascribed to the offering of Christ in heaven, which the offering of the High Priest in the Holy of Holies was appointed to produce; and that, unquestionably,

[f] Heb. ix. 23. [g] Heb. x. 14. [h] Serm. III. p. 74.

is, the *confecration* of thofe who partake of its falutary influence.

And as, by the miniftry of the High Prieft, the Ifraelites were qualified for the worfhip of the Tabernacle, fo likewife, through the offering made by Jefus Chrift, we obtain permiffion to approach the prefence of God, and to ferve him with acceptance. St. Paul affures us, that through Chrift " we have *accefs* unto " the Father [i];" and again, that in him " we " have boldnefs, and *accefs* with confidence[k]:" and in this Epiftle to the Hebrews, the confideration that " we have a great High Prieft, " that is paffed into the heavens, Jefus the Son " of God," is held out as an encouragement to us to " *come* boldly to the throne of grace[l]." And again in the tenth chapter, the Apoftle, at the conclufion of his difcourfe upon the Priefthood of Chrift, and the benefits which we derive from it, exhorts us to " *draw near* " with a true heart, in full affurance of faith[m]." From all which it is manifeft that Jefus Chrift is to us, under the Gofpel, what the High Prieft was to the Ifraelites of old. By his office and miniftry in the heavenly Taber-

[i] Eph. ii. 18. [k] Eph. iii. 12.
[l] Heb. iv. 14, 16. [m] Heb. x. 22.

nacle, he fanctified and confecrated the whole Chriftian Church, and hath obtained for all the members of it the glorious privilege of accefs to God.

But while, upon the authority of the Apoftle, we thus maintain a correfpondence between Chrift, in his prieftly character, and the legal High Prieft, let us not forget that the chief defign of this Epiftle to the Hebrews, is to fhew that the miniftry which Chrift hath obtained, is more excellent than that to which they were called who ferved the Tabernacle. Accordingly, in the courfe of this Epiftle we find enumerated a variety of circumftances, in which this fuperior excellency confifts. By following the Apoftle in this part of his argument, while we confirm the point concerning which we are more immediately enquiring, we fhall at the fame time acquire a more diftinct view of the whole doctrine under confideration, and be able to afcertain, with greater clearnefs, the nature of thofe benefits which our great High Prieft hath obtained for us.

Now one circumftance, upon which is founded the fuperior excellency of Chrift's priefthood priesthood above that of the legal Priests, is, *the continuance and unchangeableness of his office.* " Thou," says the Apostle, applying to our Lord the words of the royal Prophet, in the hundred and tenth Psalm, " thou art a Priest " for ever, after the order of Melchisedeck [n]." The law making men High Priests which had infirmitiy [o], there was of necessity a perpetual change of the person who filled the office. " They," that is, the High Priests of the order of Aaron, " were not suffered to conti- " nue, by reason of death [p]:" consequently they were many in number, succeeding each other in a continued series, till at length the whole order was changed and abolished, by the establishment of that priesthood which it typified and prefigured [q]. But the priesthood of our Lord is without succession or change: he is in reality what Melchisedeck, from the silence of the Scriptures respecting him, is said to be, " a Priest for ever." With respect to Melchisedeck, we read of no Priest who went before him in the order to which he belonged, nor of any by whom he was succeeded. In his priesthood he stands singly and alone; nor

[n] Heb. vii. 17. [o] Heb. vii. 28.
[p] Heb. vii. 23. [q] Heb. vii. 11, 12.

is any thing recorded respecting his genealogy or family, his parentage or birth, his admission to the priesthood, or his removal from it by death; on which account he is said by the Apostle to be " without father, without mo-
" ther, and without descent;" to have " nei-
" ther beginning of days, nor end of life,"
but to abide " a Priest continually [r]." In like manner the priesthood of our Lord is unchangeable, and without end. He is " a Priest
" for ever," and will throughout all ages continue to exercise his ministry for the benefit of that Church, which he hath purchased with his own blood; and having an unchangeable priesthood, " he is able to save them to the
" uttermost, that come unto God by him,
" seeing he ever liveth to make intercession
" for them [s]."

Another circumstance, on account of which the priesthood of our Lord is more excellent than that of the sons of Aaron, is, *the superior efficacy of his ministry*. By a *single* offering he consecrated at once, and for ever, his whole Church, so as to include not only the individual members of whom it was then composed,

[r] Heb. vii. 3.   [s] Heb. vii. 24, 25.

SERMON IV.

but likewife all who fhould, in after times, be ingrafted into it by baptifm: or, to ufe the words of the Apoftle, " by *one* offering he " hath perfected *for ever* them that are " fanctified'." But this the legal High Priefts could not do. " The law," fays the Apoftle, " having a fhadow of good things to " come, and not the very image of the things, " can never, with thofe facrifices which they " offered year by year continually, make the " comers thereunto perfect ":" or rather, as the paffage fhould be tranflated, " cannot, " with thofe facrifices which they offer *year* " *by year*, make perfect *for ever*," that is, confecrate for ever, " thofe who come unto " God," viz. the worfhippers of the Tabernacle. And the infufficiency of the legal economy in this refpect, the Apoftle proceeds to argue from the continual repetition of thefe facrifices. " For then would they not have " ceafed to be offered?" Yes, verily: for to what purpofe fhould that be repeated, which has already anfwered the end propofed? Whence the neceffity of an annual purifica-

---
t Heb. x. 14.
u Σκιαν γαρ εχων ο νομος των μελλοντων αγαθων, ουκ αυτην την εικονα των πραγματων, κατ' ενιαυτον ταις αυταις θυσιαις, ας προσφερουσιν, εις το διηνεκες ουδεποτε δυναται τες προσερχομενες τελειωσαι. Heb. x. 1.

tion,

tion, if the worshippers, by *one* offering, had been consecrated *for ever*? And of this the worshippers themselves would not have been ignorant: because that being " once purged," or, rather, being *completely* purged by *one* offering [w], they would " have had no more con-" science of sins;" they would not have been conscious that any further offering was necessary to cleanse and prepare them for the worship of God. But, on the other hand, they well knew that their peculiar privileges were not conferred by a perpetual gift, but were granted only for a year; at the expiration of which their covenant would be void, unless renewed in the appointed manner; and they themselves would revert to their original incapacity of approaching the Divine presence, unless qualified afresh by a reconsecration. And therefore in these legal sacrifices there was " a " remembrance again made of sins every year.

[w] ἅπαξ κεκαθαρμενους—The Apostle in another place uses a similar expression. " Who needeth not daily, as those " High Priests, to offer up sacrifice, first for his own sins, " and then for the people's; for this he did *once*, when he " offered up himself." " Semel, εφαπαξ. Magna est hoc " in loco, et aliis deinceps pluribus, hujus adverbii em-" phasis. Significat enim quod semel factum est, ita abso-" lutum fuisse, ut repetere nullo modo sit necesse." Bezæ Annot. in Heb. vii. 27.

" For

SERMON IV.

" For it is not poffible that the blood of bulls
" and of goats fhould take away fins [x];" that
is, fhould take them away completely and for
ever. It had no fuch power in its own nature, nor had it received any fuch from the
appointment of God. But what the legal
offerings could only do by an *annual repetition,*
Chrift, by *one* offering, effected *for ever.*
" By his own blood he entered in *once* into
" the holy place, having obtained *eternal* re-
" demption for us [y]." " For Chrift is not
" entered into the holy places made with
" hands," into the earthly Tabernacle erected
by Mofes, " but into heaven itfelf, now to
" appear in the prefence of God for us; nor
" yet that he fhould offer himfelf *often*, as
" the High Prieft entereth into the holy
" place, *every year* with blood of others: (for
" then muft he often have fuffered fince the
" foundation of the world) but now *once*
" in the end of the world, hath he appeared
" to put away fin by the facrifice of him-
" felf [z]." " And every Prieft ftandeth *daily*
" (that is, on every day of expiation [a]),
" miniftering

[x] Heb. x. 1—4.   [y] Heb. ix. 12.   [z] Heb. ix. 24—26.
 [a] Commentators, in general, underftand the Apoftle to
fpeak in this place either of the daily facrifice, properly fo
called,

" ministering and offering oftentimes the
" same sacrifices, which can never take away
" sins;

called, or of those occasional sacrifices for sin, for the offering of which, among other things, the Priests, in the order of their courses, attended *daily* in the sanctuary. But I am rather of opinion that he continues to discourse of the *annual* sacrifice, offered by the High Priest in the Holy of Holies; with which, in the beginning of this chapter, he had compared the offering of Christ. And in this I join with Socinus, who observes, that the expression *daily* does not here signify *on every day,* but *at a certain stated time continually.* And in support of this observation, he refers us to chap. vii. 27. where the Apostle uses this very expression in the same sense. " Who needeth not *daily,* as those High
" Priests, to offer up sacrifice, first for his own sins, and
" then for the people's." " Quotidie dicit; cum tamen
" id fieret a Sacerdotibus semel tantum quotannis. Nusquam
" enim legitur, summum Sacerdotem in sacrificiis, quæ pro
" populo fiebant, pro se etiam offerre debuisse, nisi in sa-
" crificio illo anniversario." De Servatore, par. ii. cap. xvi.

Grotius, in contending for the common interpretation, thus opposes the argument of Socinus. " Sic et cap. x. 11.
" quotidiana sacrificia cum Christi sacrificio comparantur:
" cujus loci sententiam evertit Socinus *quotidie* exponens
" *quotannis*, nullo exemplo. Nam quod locum Heb. vii.
" 27. adfert huic interpretationi firmandæ, frustra est, cum
" falso sumat Sacerdotem in solo anniversario sacrificio pro
" se offerre debuisse. Contra enim pro se offerre debuit,
" quoties peccati sibi erat conscius. Lev. iv. 3." De Satisfactione Christi, cap. x.

The reply of Crellius is as follows: " In loco citato,
" cap. x. de sacrificio anniversario sermonem esse, satis do-
" cere

SERMON IV.

" sins;" or, which can by no means take away sins for ever. " But this man, after
" he

" cere poffunt ea, quæ ab ipfo capitis initio leguntur; unde
" cætera, quæ hoc loco dicuntur, pendere, præter rem ip-
" fam, Beza in fua verfione oftendit. Inftitutam enim
" effe a divino auctore collationem inter folenne facrifi-
" cium expiatorium, et facrificium Chrifti, verf. 1. et 3.
" aperte comprobant. Particulam illam καθ' ἡμέραν non
" fimpliciter explicat Socinus per vocem *quotannis*, fed
" *certo quodam tempore perpetuo*, ut eo loco, quem Grotius
" citavit, videre eft, h. e. certo quodam die quotannis. Hoc
" vero nec fine exemplo fecit Socinus, nec, fi exemplum
" deeffet, protinus repudiari deberet, cum rationem hujus
" fuæ interpretationis attulerit, quod de anniverfario facri-
" ficio hucufque inftitutus effet fermo, quod veram obla-
" tionis Chrifti umbram fuiffe antea docuerat. Quod ad
" locum cap. vii. 27. attinet, in quo exemplum ejus figni-
" ficationis extare Socinus ftatuit, non dicit Socinus, fum-
" mum Sacerdotem *in folo anniverfario facrificio* pro fe of-
" ferre debuiffe; fed ita fcribit: *Nufquam legitur fummum
" Sacerdotem in facrificiis, quæ pro populo fiebant, pro fe
" etiam offerre debuiffe, nifi in facrificio illo anniverfario.*
" In facrificiis igitur quæ *pro populo fiebant*, debuiffe pro
" fe etiam offerre fummum Sacerdotem, nifi in illo anni-
" verfario, nufquam legi fcribit Socinus: non vero, eum
" pro fe feparatim offerre non debuiffe, cum fibi delicti
" alicujus effet confcius. Id autem rectiffime urget Soci-
" nus, quia Auctor D. loco d. cap. vii. manifefte facit
" mentionem facrificii, quod pro populo fieret, in quo Sa-
" cerdos prius pro fe, tum demum pro populo offerre debu-
" erit. Ita enim ait : *Qui* (Pontifex nofter Chriftus) *non
" habet quotidie neceffe, quemadmodum illi Pontifices, prius
" pro*

SERMON IV.

"he had offered one sacrifice for sin, for ever
"sat down on the right hand of God;
"from henceforth expecting till his enemies
"be made his footstool. For by one offer-
"ing he hath perfected for ever them that
"are sanctified [b]." From all which we may
collect, that Christ, having once entered into
the heavenly Tabernacle, abideth there continually, and by his prevailing intercession obtains for his Church the continued enjoyment of that glorious privilege, which he purchased with his blood.

"*pro propriis peccatis victimas offerre, deinde* (pro pecca-
"tis) *populi. Hoc enim fecit semel cum seipsum obtulit.*
"Adde quod ne sic quidem, si Grotium sequamur, Sacer-
"dos quotidie offerre debuerit, non magis quam alius qui-
"vis e populo. Neque enim quotidie peccati alicujus sibi
"erat conscius, pro quo offerre deberet, alias idem de quo-
"libet Israelita dicendum esset. Quapropter rectissime
"statuit Socinus de anniversario sacrificio ibi esse sermo-
"nem, ac proinde vocem *quotidie* ita interpretandam esse,
"ac si dictum esset, certo quodam die quotannis." Re-
sponsio ad lib. H. Grotii de Satisfac. cap. x.

On the same side I may cite the authority of Dr. Ham-
mond, who renders καθ' ἡμεραν, *upon a day*, i, e. as he maintains in his Paraphrase, *upon the day of expiation.*

It may be added, in further support of this interpretation,
that some MSS of note read Και πας μεν αρχιερευς ιστηκε καθ'
ἡμεραν, &c. and every *High* Priest standeth daily, &c. (see
Wetsten) which reading is adopted by Grotius.

[b] Heb. x. 11—14.

The

The ministry which Christ hath obtained is also more excellent than that of the Priests who served the Tabernacle, " by how much " he is the Mediator of a better covenant, " which was established upon better pro-" mises [c]." He is the Mediator of a better covenant; a covenant which admits us to a nearer and more intimate communion with God, and to the participation of greater and more important benefits. The Israelites were indeed admitted into the presence of God; but they approached him with fear and trembling; and, though he condescended to be called their God, he ruled them with the severity of an avenging Judge, rather than with the kindness of a compassionate Parent. But to us he appears in a milder character: we have not received the spirit of bondage unto fear; but we have received the spirit of adoption: God hath taken us into his family, and hath permitted us to approach him with the tender appellation of Father [d]. The throne of the great King is no longer surrounded with the tremendous ensigns of terrible majesty; but is a throne of grace, to which in all our sins, and all our wants, we may boldly

[c] Heb. viii. 6. [d] Rom. viii. 15.

apply,

apply, in the fullest confidence of being heard, forgiven, and relieved. " Let us," says the Apostle, " come boldly to the throne of " grace, that we may obtain mercy, and find " grace to help in time of need [e]."

And as the covenant is thus better, so are the promises better upon which it was established. Through Christ we have not only access to God in the Church militant here upon earth, but we are encouraged to hope for nearer approaches to the Divine presence hereafter, in the Church triumphant in heaven. And, in this respect, the privilege conferred upon the Christian Church infinitely exceeds all that the Israelites enjoyed through the ministry of their High Priest. The promises made to them were wholly of a temporal nature; and the utmost which their covenant taught them to expect, was the possession, in peace and prosperity, of that good land, which God had promised to their fathers. But to the Christian Church the promises run in a higher strain: we look for a better country than was that of Canaan; even an heavenly one: and are taught to expect, not so much temporal peace and prosperity, as the enjoyment of that everlasting rest,

[e] Heb. iv. 16.

which

which remaineth to the people of God [f]. We have " boldness to enter into the holiest by " the blood of Jesus [g] :" into heaven itself, which he hath opened to all Believers; and whither he, as our forerunner, is already gone, to prepare for us mansions of bliss and glory in his father's house; and whence, agreeably to his own promise, he will come again, and receive us to himself, that where he is, there we may be also [h].

Such is the glorious privilege of the Christian Church. We have access to God, and the capacity of performing to him an acceptable service in this life; and we have the sure and certain hope of being admitted to the everlasting enjoyment of him in the life to come. Nor let any sincere Believer despair of obtaining, through the intercession of his Saviour, the actual possession of that immortal happiness, to which the privilege, enjoyed by the Church upon earth, is merely preparatory. Is he alarmed by a sense of his own corruption, and a dread of the Divine vengeance? Let him remember, that in heaven Jesus Christ, the High Priest of our profession, continually appears for us in the presence of God; where he undertakes our cause, in-

---

[f] Heb. iv. 9.   [g] Heb. x. 19.   [h] John xiv. 2, 3.

terposes

terpofes in our behalf, and obtains for us pardon of our fins, and peace with God. " If any man fin, we have an advocate with the Father, Jefus Chrift the righteous [i] :" and fo prevailing is the interceffion of our heavenly Advocate, that St. Paul boldly defies all the enemies of our falvation to oppofe its influence. " Who fhall lay any thing to the charge of God's elect? It is God that juftifieth: who is he that condemneth? It is Chrift that died, yea rather that is rifen again, who is even at the right hand of God, who alfo maketh interceffion for us [k]." And in this Epiftle to the Hebrews, the interceffion of our Redeemer is made the ground of our hope and confidence in him. " Wherefore he is able to fave them to the uttermoft that come unto God by him, feeing he ever liveth to make interceffion for them [l]."

The truth of the general pofition, which I undertook to prove in this Difcourfe, is, I truft, by this time fufficiently manifeft. We have feen that the Scriptures contain many general affertions of our Lord's prieftly cha-

[i] 1 John ii. 1.   [k] Rom. viii. 33.   [l] Heb. vii. 25.

racter, afcribing to him both the title of Prieft, and alfo the peculiar functions of the priefthood: and that, in fpeaking of his priefthood, they contain particular references to the legal High Prieft, and to the functions difcharged by him on the feaft of expiation; exprefsly declaring, that as the High Prieft offered the blood of the bullock and the goat in that holy place upon earth, where God vouchfafed a vifible manifeftation of his glorious prefence, and by his offering fanctified the Ifraelites, and gave them a title to the temporal bleffings of their covenant; fo Chrift offered his own blood in heaven itfelf, where the Divine glory fhines forth in the fulnefs of its fplendor, that by his offering he might fanctify his Church, and make us capable of attaining thofe fpiritual and eternal promifes, held out to us in the Gofpel: and from the whole we hefitate not to infer, that an office and miniftry is attributed to our bleffed Lord in heaven, correfponding to that which was antiently difcharged by the Levitical Priefts in the earthly Tabernacle.

And here I fhall beg leave to clofe the Scripture-evidence, by which the doctrine of Atonement is fupported: and have accordingly

ingly now completed what I have to offer upon the firſt of the two general heads, into which, at the commencement of theſe Diſcourſes, I diſtributed my ſubject.

Under the ſecond general head, I propoſed to conſider the principal objections, which the Opponents of this doctrine, and eſpecially the Hiſtorian of the Corruptions of Chriſtianity, have urged againſt it. Theſe objections may alſo be reduced to two heads, according as the intention of our adverſaries is, either to invalidate the ſcriptural proofs of the doctrine in queſtion, by attributing to the ſacred writers a ſenſe, different from that for which we contend; or, ſecondly, to oppoſe the doctrine in a more direct and poſitive manner, by ſhewing that it makes no part of that ſcheme of religion which is delivered to us in the Scriptures.

I ſhall begin with the objections of the former claſs; and ſhall accordingly, in the next Diſcourſe, endeavour to vindicate the ſacred text from the attempts which have been made, by Socinian writers, to pervert its meaning.

SERMON V.

1 Cor. xiii. 12.

Now we see through a glass, darkly.

IN the preceding Lectures it has been my endeavour to shew, that the doctrine of Atonement, by the blood of Christ, is contained in the Scriptures: and in proof of this position, I have collected from the various books of Scripture a multitude of passages, forming altogether a body of evidence so uniform and consistent, and so decisive of the point in question, as apparently to leave not the least room for cavil or dispute.

But it not uncommonly happens, that the greatest discord prevails, where the most perfect harmony might have been expected. The passions and prejudices of men close their eyes against the clearest light, and make them eager to dispute against the plainest and most evident truths; nor is there any truth, however plain and evident, which a sophist will not contrive to bring into question. And thus it has happened in the case before us. To the doctrine of Atonement, the testimony borne by the word of God, is, as we have seen, most full and express. And yet, notwithstanding this testimony, we find a determined Adversary hardy enough to come forward with the professed intention of shewing, that the whole doctrine is of human invention, and has no countenance whatever in the Scriptures[a]. In vain do we oppose to this bold assertion, the many positive declarations with which the books of Scripture abound. He cannot indeed deny the existence of these declarations; but he contrives to elude their force, and by sophistical expositions to render them less adverse to the opinions of his sect.

In the following Discourse, I propose to consider the general method of interpretation employed for this purpose; and shall endeavour to shew, that it is adopted on the present occasion without authority, and in direct opposition to the manifest intention of the sacred Writers.

[a] Hist. of Cor. vol. i. p. 153.

Among

SERMON V.

Among the passages of Scripture adduced to prove the doctrine of Atonement, we depend with peculiar confidence upon those, which denominate the death of Christ *a sacrifice* and *a sin-offering*, and which assert of his blood, that it is our *ransom*, and the *price of our redemption*. And it must be owned, that the obvious sense of all such expressions is so strongly in favour of this doctrine, that at first view one would think it extremely difficult, if not utterly impossible, by any means to evade their force. But, great as the difficulty appears, a Socinian readily surmounts it, by the bare assumption, that the language of Scripture is, on such occasions, merely *figurative*. Thus the Historian of the Corruptions of Christianity admits, without hesitation, that the death of Christ is called in Scripture *a sacrifice* and *a sin-offering:* but then he affirms, that these, and such like expressions, are to be *figuratively* interpreted; and that, being so interpreted, they do not oblige us to believe that Christ died a sacrifice in any other manner, than as any person may be said to be a sacrifice to the cause in which he dies [b]. " In " every sacrifice," says he, " the victim is

[a] Hist. of Cor. v. i. p. 278.

" slain

" slain for the benefit of the perſon on whoſe
" account it is offered; ſo Chriſt, dying to pro-
" cure the greateſt poſſible benefit to the hu-
" man race, is ſaid to have given his life *a ſa-*
" *crifice* for us: and moreover, as the end of
" the Goſpel is to promote the reformation of
" ſinners, in order to procure the pardon of
" ſin, the death of Chriſt is more expreſsly
" compared to *a ſin-offering* [b]." And he contends, that theſe points of reſemblance between the death of Chriſt and the Jewiſh ſacrifices, ſufficiently juſtify and explain the language of the Scriptures relating to it, without
ſuppoſing that the ſacrifices, preſcribed in the
Jewiſh law, are *types* of Chriſt's ſacrifice, or
aſcribing to the death of Chriſt any *immediate*
power of making expiation for ſin, and of
procuring pardon. And ſpeaking of Iſaiah's
prophecy, " Thou ſhalt make his ſoul an of-
" fering for ſin [c]," he affirms, that, even allowing the propriety of our tranſlation, " it
" cannot be proved to exhibit any thing more
" than *a figurative alluſion* [d]." So again, he
admits that Chriſt is ſaid to have given his
life *a ranſom* for us: he neverthelefs denies
that we derive any benefit *immediately* from

[b] Hiſt. of Cor. v. i. p. 182.   [c] Iſ. liii. 10.
[d] Hiſt. of Cor. v. i. p. 184.

his

SERMON V.

his death; nor will he allow us to confider the giving of his life as a *real* price paid for our deliverance from death; but he afferts, that this expreffion is *figuratively* applied to Chrift, becaufe he died in confequence of having voluntarily, and for the love which he bore to us, undertaken the work of our falvation [e]. And in another place he affirms, that the death of Chrift may be called *a facrifice for fin*, and *a ranfom*; and alfo that Chrift may, in a general way, be faid to have *died in our ftead*, and to have *borne our fins*: and that *figurative* language, even ftronger than this, may be ufed by perfons, who do not confider the death of Chrift as having any immediate relation to the forgivenefs of fins; but believe only, that it was a neceffary circumftance in the fcheme of the Gofpel, and that this fcheme was neceffary to reform the world [f]. And thus, by this pretence of *a figure*, he endeavours, moft unwarrantably, to evade the true fenfe of Scripture, and to fet afide as infignificant, and without force, the plaineft and moft pofitive texts, againft which, if fairly interpreted, his favourite hypothefis could not be maintained.

It will affift us in our inveftigation of this

[e] Hift. of Cor. v. i. p. 202.   [f] Ibid. p. 214.

method of interpretation, by which the senfe of Scripture is thus evaded, and explained away, if we firft afcertain what our Hiftorian underftands by *figurative language*.

From the foregoing quotations it appears, that the *figurative* fenfe of an expreffion is oppofed to its *literal* and *proper* fenfe; and that an expreffion becomes *figurative*, when it is transferred from the thing of which it is *properly* fignificant, to fome other thing, on account of fome refemblance which they bear, or are fuppofed to bear, to each other. Thus, by way of example, a *lion* is properly an animal, whofe characteriftic quality is courage. But a man, who poffeffes this quality in an eminent degree, fo far refembles a lion, and is figuratively called by that name. Thus alfo *thirft* is properly a painful fenfation, arifing from a drynefs of the throat, and occafioning an eager defire of drink. But there is in a *dry foil* an aptnefs to receive moifture with facility, fomewhat refembling that eagernefs for drink, which characterizes a thirfty animal; and therefore a *dry* land is figuratively called a *thirfty* land. Thus again, a victim devoted to death, and actually flain, and offered to God, in order to procure for the offerer the Divine favour and acceptance, is

properly

properly *a sacrifice:* but the man who, in order to attain any end, exposes himself to such danger, that his death is the inevitable consequence, bears some resemblance to the former, and may therefore figuratively be called a *sacrifice* to the cause in which he dies.

And hence it further appears, that the signification of figurative language does not arise from *the real nature of the thing to which it is transferred,* but only from *the imagination of him who transfers it:* and accordingly it does not express what is *true* and *real* in the thing itself; but is applied by way of *allusion* merely; for the sake perhaps of a rhetorical flourish, and in order to express a thing in a more striking and forcible manner. Thus the *real* nature of a lion belongs not to a courageous man: but because the quality which principally characterizes the former animal, exists in an eminent degree in the latter, therefore the imagination conceives them to be, what they really are not, partakers of one common nature, and applies to them one common name. Thus also in a dry land there is only an *imaginary* thirst: there is *really* no eagerness, no desire whatever; only its aptness to receive moisture with facility, is

conceived

conceived by the imagination to be of the fame kind with that eager defire of drink which is properly *thirſt*, and is therefore called by the fame name. So alfo in the giving up of one's life for the fupport of any caufe, the oblation, on account of which it is called a facrifice, is not *real*, but *imaginary:* there is a mere expofure of a man's life to danger, and it may be to inevitable lofs, which the imagination conceives to be of the fame kind with that oblation which is neceffary to a proper facrifice; and therefore the life fo expofed and loft, is alfo faid to be *facrificed*.

It is the opinion of this Author, that language, if it cannot be *literally* interpreted, is neceffarily of the *figurative* kind here defcribed, applied only by way of *allufion*; and not to exprefs any *truth* or *reality*. And accordingly he argues, that where the words of Scripture will not admit of a literal fenfe (as on fome occafions they undeniably will not), we muft then have recourfe to a figure. But this is a miftake. For there is a fpecies of language, ufually called *analogical*; which, though not ftrictly *proper*, is far from being merely *figurative:* fince in this cafe the name of one thing is transferred to another, on account, not of *an imaginary refemblance*, but of

a real

a real correspondence: or, in other words, the translation is made, not because *the things themselves* are similar, but because they are in similar *relations*. For, agreeably to the definition of the Mathematicians, *analogy* is the similitude of relations: and is said to take place, when the first of four magnitudes has the same ratio, or relation, to the second, which the third has to the fourth. Now *analogical* language arises from a similitude of this kind. For when there subsists between two things the same relation as between some other two, then, on account of this analogy, the name which properly belongs to one of the terms in one relation, is frequently transferred to its corresponding term in the other relation; and is as truly significant of the *real* nature of the thing in the relation in which it stands, as it could be were it the primitive and proper word.

Permit me to illustrate my meaning by an example.—Our blessed Lord is called in Scripture the *head* of the Church [s]. Now the term *head* is not here to be understood in a strictly *literal* and *proper* sense: for literally and properly the *head* is the uppermost and

[s] Eph. v. 23.

principal

principal part of an animal; the organ of fenfation; and the fource from which all the other parts derive motion, and the power of performing their refpective functions. Nor is it merely *figurative*, fignificant of nothing real, but applied only by way of allufion. It is *analogical:* for between Chrift and his Church there is the fame relation, as between the head and the body: and fince what a literal and proper head is to the animal frame, that Chrift is to his Church; therefore, on account of this analogy, he is called the *head* of his Church: and the office which he fuftains with refpect to his Church, is as truly expreffed by this *analogical* term, as it would be by any *proper* word which could have been employed. The Church is in like manner, and on the fame account, called the *body of Chrift,* that is, the body of which Chrift is the head. And not only fo, but becaufe Chriftians are to the Church, what members are to the body, the individuals who compofe the Church, are further called *members* of Chrift's body [h].

It will be found, upon examination, that all languages are full of thefe *analogical* terms.

[h] 1 Cor. xii. 27.

Even

Even *senfible* objects are not unfrequently denominated by words borrowed from other senfible objects, with which we are better acquainted, or more immediately concerned. Thus the term *foot* properly fignifies the lower extremity of *an animal*, or that on which the animal ftands. But becaufe the lower extremity or bafe of *a mountain*, is to the mountain what the *foot* is to an animal, it is therefore called by the fame name: and the term, thus applied, is fignificant of fomething *real*; fomething, which, if not a foot in ftrict propriety of fpeech, is neverthelefs truly fo, confidered with refpect to the circumftance upon which the analogy is founded.

But this mode of expreffion is more common with refpect to our *mental* and *intellectual* faculties and operations; which we are wont to denominate by words borrowed from fimilar functions of the bodily organs, and correfponding attributes of material things. Thus to *fee*, is properly to acquire impreffions of *fenfible* objects by the organ of fight: but to the *mind* is alfo attributed an eye, with which we are analogically faid to fee objects *intellectual*. In like manner *great* and *little*, *equal* and *unequal*, *fmooth* and *rough*, *fweet* and *four*, are properly attributes of *material* fubftances:

but

but they are analogically afcribed to fuch as are *immaterial:* for, without intending a figure, we fpeak of a great *mind* and a little *mind*; and the *natural temper* of one man is faid to be equal, fmooth, and fweet; while that of another is denominated unequal, rough, and four. And if we thus exprefs fuch *intellectual* things as fall more immediately under our obfervation, and may accordingly be contemplated with greater accuracy and attention, we cannot wonder that things *purely fpiritual* and *divine*, which are far removed from our immediate and direct infpection, fhould be exhibited to our apprehenfion after the fame manner. Indeed there is no other way by which they could be exhibited with effect: for it is only by analogical reprefentations that we can form the leaft conception of the things relating to God and the invifible world. We can have no direct and immediate idea or conception of thefe things; for they are not objects of fenfe, nor do they make any part of that which pafles within our own breafts. But material things, and the powers and operations of our own mind, furnifh us with analogies by which we may, in fome degree, conceive the nature of that Being who is infinite, and of thofe things
• which

which are spiritual and heavenly. And the conceptions which we thus form, however imperfect and inadequate, are, nevertheless, as far as they extend, just and true: consequently the language in which they are expressed, although borrowed, is not merely figurative; but is significant of something real in the nature of the things conceived.

Before I apply what has been said, to the point more immediately in question, it may not be improper to state a few instances, in which the analogy contended for may plainly be discerned, and will hardly be denied.

The anger of God, is an expression which frequently occurs in the Scriptures. But are we to understand it *literally?* It were impious to do so: for the divine Being is without passions; and therefore cannot be subject to anger, properly so called. Is then the expression merely *figurative*, and without meaning? By no means: that were to take away one of the strongest restraints upon our corrupt inclinations. Is it not rather *analogical*; intended to give us some conception of a perfection in the Divine nature, by referring us to something in our own, to which it corresponds? In man it is the passion of anger which

which prompts him, upon receiving a provocation, to punish the offender. Now there is in the Divine nature a perfection, which inclines the Deity to punish those who wilfully transgress his laws. And since this perfection, though not properly anger, is nevertheless to God, what anger is to man, on account of this analogy the Scriptures have called it by the same name: and in so doing have given us to understand, that the same severity which an angry man, possessed of power to execute his will, would shew to those who had provoked his vengeance, we may expect from God, who is infinite in power, if we wilfully sin against him.

God is also said to be *compassionate* and *merciful*. Certainly not in a *literal* and *proper* sense. But the Scriptures by these expressions give us to understand, that, if not compassion and mercy properly so called, there are, nevertheless, in the Divine nature perfections corresponding to these feelings, which incline the Deity to relieve the wants, and to forgive the sins, of his miserable and offending creatures. And we are hence assured, that if we make our distresses known unto God, and with a true penitent heart, and lively faith, turn unto him, we shall experience

perience from him that lenity and kindness, which, in a corresponding situation, a merciful and compassionate fellow-creature would be disposed to shew us.

In like manner *the rewards and punishments of the other world* are described by the sacred writers in terms and phrases, which are properly significant of such joys and torments as are wont most sensibly to affect us in our *present* state: not to furnish us with any direct and positive knowledge of the invisible world; for of this we are not capable; but by analogical representations to give us some conception of what we are to expect hereafter; a conception, remote indeed and inadequate; sufficient, however, to excite our hopes, and to alarm our fears; to quicken our diligence in the great work of our salvation; and to induce us, by a suitable behaviour in this our time of trial, to prepare for that awful day, when we shall appear before the tribunal of the great Judge, " who will render to every " man according to his deeds [1]."

The foregoing instances, in which the analogy is evident and undeniable, will assist us

[1] Rom. ii. 6.

in giving a right interpretation to thofe paffages of Scripture, which immediately relate to our prefent fubject.

And firft, the *blood,* or *life,* of Chrift is called in Scripture our *ranfom,* and the *price of our redemption.* Now, admitting that thefe expreffions are not to be underftood *literally,* does it follow that they contain mere *figure* and *allufion?* By no means: they contain *truth* and *reality.* They are *analogical* expreffions, ufed by the facred writers to give us fome conception of the method, by which we are delivered from the punifhment of fin by Jefus Chrift. We know the mifery of a ftate of bondage and captivity: and under this view we are taught in Scripture to confider the natural ftate of man: he is " fold under " fin [k];" is " the fervant of fin [l];" is under the power and dominion of the Devil, by whom he is " taken captive at his will [m]." We further know, that one method of obtaining deliverance from captivity, is the interference of fome friend, who undertakes to *redeem* the captive, or to purchafe his freedom by the payment of a ftipulated *price* or *ranfom.* Under this character, Chrift is repre-

[k] Rom. vii. 14.   [l] Rom. vi. 17.   [m] 2 Tim. ii. 26.

fented

sented to have appeared for us. He came to redeem us from the power of sin and Satan, by paying for our deliverance no less a price than his own blood. " In him we have re-" demption through his blood [n] :" " The son " of man," says he himself, " came to give " his life a ransom for many [o];" and says St. Paul, " he gave himself a ransom for all [p]." And we are taught by this representation, that the blood of Christ, in the deliverance of sinful man, corresponds to a price or ransom in the deliverance of a captive: and consequently is a price and a ransom, if not literally and properly, at least really and truly. And this St. Peter plainly intimates, when he opposes the blood of Christ to those things which, in the dealings of men one with another, are commonly employed as ransoms, or prices of redemption. " Ye were not re-" deemed with corruptible things, as *silver* " *and gold*—but with the *precious blood of* " *Christ* [q]." Than which words language cannot declare with greater plainness and precision, that the blood of Christ is, in truth and reality, as much a price as silver and gold;

---

[n] Eph. i. 7. [o] Matt. xx. 28.
[p] 1 Tim. ii. 6. [q] 1 Pet. i. 18, 19.

only

only a price of infinitely higher value. Since, then, we are not merely said to be redeemed, but further to be redeemed with a price; and since the price of our redemption is expressly opposed to such things as among men are commonly used for that purpose; there can be in this place no room for a mere figurative sense; but we must understand the Apostle to mean, that the blood of Christ is to man, in his spiritual captivity, what silver and gold is to a real or proper captive; the price of his redemption, or that to which his deliverance is immediately owing. And this is the whole for which we contend.

It has been insinuated [r], that the expressions *price* and *ransom*, are merely figurative, upon the ground that the representations of Scripture, upon this head, are not consistent and uniform. For the price of redemption is said to have been given, not only by Christ, but also by God himself: Thus we read in St. John, that " God so loved the world, that " he gave his only begotten Son; that who- " soever believeth in him should not perish, " but have everlasting life [s]." And again in St. Paul, " he that spared not his own son,

---

[r] Hist. of Cor. p. 201.   [s] John iii. 16.

" but

" but delivered him up for us all, how shall
" he not with him freely give us all things[t]?"
Were this any real objection, it would admit
of an easy answer. For in neither of the
places alleged is God said to have given his
son as a price or ransom. " He so loved the
" world that he *gave*"—that is, gave to the
world, or sent into the world, " his only-be-
" gotten son." " He spared not his own
" son, but delivered him up for us all;" that
is, did not withhold him from us, but sent
him to pay the price of our redemption. And
thus, since God is not said to have given the
son in the same sense that the son gave himself, viz. as a ransom, we need not have recourse to a figure for reconciling this supposed inconsistency.

Attempts have also been made to with-
draw us from viewing the blood of Christ in
the light of a real price, by the consideration
of the person to whom, if a price, it ought to
have been paid. For it has been observed,
that a price must necessarily be paid to some
one: and that a ransom is always paid to
him, from whose power the captive is redeemed. And hence it has been argued, that

[t] Rom. viii. 32.

if the blood of Chrift be the price of our redemption, it muft have been paid to the *Devil*; for to him mankind had been given over in confequence of the fin of Adam. In order to obviate this apparently fhocking confequence, attempts have been made to fhew, that the price was really paid to *God*; and that the *Devil*, in this cafe, is to be confidered only as the executioner of Divine vengeance. How far this anfwer is fatisfactory, I fhall not ftay to enquire : it will be fufficient to obferve, that the argument itfelf is not well founded. For let it be confidered, that the blood of Chrift is *analogically* a price. Now the name which properly belongs to one term in an analogy, is transferred to its correfponding term, not becaufe the things expreffed by this name correfpond to each other in every poffible point ; for this is by no means neceffary ; but becaufe they correfpond in a certain refpect : nor are we required to take into confideration any circumftance, upon which the fimilitude of the relations is not founded. Now the blood of Chrift correfponds to a proper price, in the deliverance effected by it: this is the circumftance upon which the fimilitude of the relations is founded ; and therefore to this alone are we required

required to attend. Consequently the objection, arising from the consideration of the person to whom the price is paid, is nugatory and futile; inasmuch as it proceeds upon a circumstance with which we are not necessarily concerned.

Secondly. The death of Christ is frequently called in Scripture a *sacrifice* and a *sin-offering:* not, as the Socinian hypothesis asserts, *figuratively*, or merely in allusion to the Jewish sacrifices; but rather *analogically*, because the death of Christ is to the Christian Church, what the sacrifices for sin were to the worshippers of the Tabernacle. Indeed the whole Legal economy furnishes abundant matter for analogies of this kind, being so constituted and contrived by Divine wisdom, as to correspond in a variety of instances to the Christian; thus serving, in an eminent degree, to illustrate and explain its nature and design. For the Law has an entire reference to the Gospel; and was ordained, not as a distinct and separate institution, but as a state of preparation and previous instruction: to use the language of St. Paul, it is " our schoolmaster " to bring us unto Christ^a." And more

^a Gal. iii. 24.

especially

SERMON V.

especially the things in the law which have any relation to the worship of God, or were consecrated and set apart for holy purposes, were intended, not merely for the more orderly and acceptable performance of religious worship in the times then present, but also to delineate and shadow forth another state of things; to be *types* and *figures* of a better dispensation, to be established in after times.

This typical nature of the legal dispensation the Apostle himself asserts, when he says of the law, that it had " a *shadow* of good things " to come [w];" that it gave the outline, or afforded an obscure representation of those good things, which Christ, in the fulness of time, was to come and establish. To the same purpose he elsewhere affirms of the Tabernacle, and the vessels employed in the service of the Tabernacle, that they were " *patterns* of " things in the heavens [x]." And of the inner Tabernacle more especially, or the Holy of Holies, that it was a *figure* of the highest heaven [y]. And of the Priests who offered gifts and sacrifices upon earth, he declares, that they served " unto the *example* and *shadow* of hea-

---

[w] Heb. x. 1.   [x] Heb. ix. 23.
[y] Heb. ix. 24.

" venly

SERMON V. 137

"venly things [z]." And he further declares a variety of circumstances in the Legal dispensation, to which he opposes corresponding circumstances in the Christian. Thus the *earthly* and *temporary* promises of the Law are opposed to the *heavenly* and *eternal* promises of the Gospel; the *carnal* ordinances of the former, to the *spiritual* institutions of the latter: *bodily* pollution, to *mental* uncleanness; the blood of the *expiatory sacrifices*, to the blood of *Christ*; and the power of the former in cleansing the *body*, to the power of the latter in purifying the *conscience*. By all which we are sufficiently authorised to consider the Law as a *typical* dispensation, delineating and prefiguring the state of things under the Gospel. And accordingly we affirm, that the passages of Scripture which speak of Christ as a *sacrifice* and a *sin-offering*, do not contain mere *figurative* allusions to the Jewish sacrifices, but ascribe a *real* and *immediate* efficacy to Christ's death; an efficacy, corresponding to that which was antiently produced by the legal sin-offerings; since, in effect, they assert, that what a victim appointed for a sin-offering was under the old covenant, that

[z] Heb. viii. 5.

Christ

Chrift himfelf is under the new: and as the blood of the legal fin-offerings cleanfed the body, and qualified for the ceremonial worfhip prefcribed by the Law, fo the blood of Chrift purifies the confcience, and confecrates to the fpiritual fervice required in the Gofpel.

In like manner the office of Chrift is *analogically* reprefented to us by the name of *Prieft* and *High Prieft*. It has been already afferted, upon the authority of the Epiftle to the Hebrews, that the High Prieft is a type of Chrift: confequently what the High Prieft was in the Legal economy, that Chrift is in the Chriftian. Under the Law, the High Prieft was accuftomed to appear before God in the inner Tabernacle, and by an offering of blood to make an atonement for the people. Such, alfo, with refpect to the Chriftian Church, is the office of Chrift in the heavenly Tabernacle. Having fuffered, as an expiatory victim, upon the crofs, he afcended into heaven, where he is reprefented as appearing for us in the prefence of God, and, by an offering of his own blood, making reconciliation for fins. Not that this reprefentation obliges us to fuppofe that Chrift, upon his afcenfion into heaven, literally fprinkled

his

his own blood in the prefence of God, as the High Prieft fprinkled the blood of the fin-offerings before the mercy-feat; but it gives us moft affuredly to underftand, that his interpofition in our behalf is attended with a *true* and *real* effect, correfponding to that which was produced by the miniftry of the High Prieft in the earthly Tabernacle: that as by the latter the Ifraelites were fanctified, and admitted to the enjoyment of the temporal bleffings of their covenant, fo by the former the members of the Chriftian Church obtain remiffion of fins, and are made partakers of the fpiritual bleffings promifed in the Gofpel.

Chrift is alfo faid *to make interceffion for us*, and *to be our Advocate with the Father*. I formerly fhewed[a] that Chrift, by virtue of his prieftly office, is neceffarily an *Interceffor* for his people, and their *Advocate* with God: fo that thefe reprefentations are not really different from that which has been already confidered. But fuppofing them to be diftinct and feparate, they will neverthelefs ftill be found perfectly confiftent both with it, and with each other. In ftrict propriety to *make*

[a] Serm. IV.

interceffion

interceſſion for a perſon, is to interpoſe in his behalf, for the purpoſe of reconciling him to one with whom he is at variance: and he is *an Advocate*, who pleads the cauſe of another in a court of judicature. Now we having, by ſin, offended God, he is repreſented as at variance with us upon this account, and as having caſt us out of his favour. And Chriſt is repreſented as interpoſing in our behalf, and undertaking our cauſe, that he might obtain of his heavenly Father to be reconciled unto us. We muſt not indeed imagine that Chriſt *literally* pleads our cauſe, or in moving and perſuaſive language intreats his heavenly Father to forego his anger, and to receive us again to favour: but the interpoſition of Chriſt, if not literally and properly interceſſion, is, neverthelefs, analogous to it; for what a proper interceſſor is between one man and another, that Chriſt is between God and man: and what a proper advocate is before a human judge, that Chriſt is in the preſence of God: it is by his intervention that we are reconciled to God: it is by his agency that we are acquitted and diſcharged; and therefore he is truly and really our Interceſſor and Advocate, if not literally, and in ſtrict propriety of ſpeech.

Thus,

SERMON V.

Thus, in variety of language, do the sacred writers represent both the efficacy of Chrift's death, and also the nature of his interposition between God and man. It has, indeed, been contended, that these different representations are themselves an argument for a figurative sense; because that otherwise the sacred writers are juftly chargeable with inconsistency in calling the same thing by different names. " If," asks the Historian of the Corruptions of Christianity,- " if one of the re-
" presentations be real, and the rest figura-
" tive, how are we to distinguish among
" them, when the writers themselves give us
" no intimation of any such difference [b]?" I answer, if these representations are all, as we affirm, analogical, it will follow that they are all real; that is, that they all exprefs some truth and reality. And thus the whole objection falls to the ground.

But I wish to meet the objection fairly, and not to take advantage of an inaccurate expression. For, unquestionably, by *real*, our Historian, in this place, means *proper*; and his argument, juftly stated, would run thus: Since of many different representations only

[b] Hift. of Cor. p. 192.

one

one can be proper, and in that cafe the reſt muſt be figurative. how are we to diſtinguiſh among them ? how are we to diſcover which is the proper repreſentation, when the writers themſelves give us no intimation of any ſuch difference ? And aſſuming that this cannot be done, he infers, that they are all figurative alike. To this I reply, that, of many different repreſentations, it is not neceſſary either that one ſhould be proper, and the reſt figurative, or that all ſhould be figurative alike. They may be (and we contend that they are) all analogical ; and then they may (and we contend that they do) all expreſs the ſame truth and reality, only under different names. Nor are the ſacred writers any more chargeable with inconſiſtency on this account, than they would have been, had they illuſtrated the ſame thing by different figures. And I would obſerve in general, that the objections, urged by Socinian writers againſt the literal and proper ſenſe of the expreſſions which we have now been conſidering, are not more favourable to their interpretation, than to that for which we contend ; which has this further advantage, that, while it is agreeable to the uſual, and indeed the only method by which Divine knowledge is, or can be communicated to man,

SERMON V. 143

man, it affords a clear and confiftent fenfe, not arbitrarily impofed, but plainly fuggefted by the words themfelves, and manifeftly intended by the facred writers: whereas the method of our adverfary is arbitrary and unlimited, and evidently intended not fo much to explain the real meaning of the facred writers, as to make them fpeak a language not wholly incompatible with his own hypothefis.

But befides this perverfion of the facred text, by the arbitrary impofition of a figurative fenfe, the fame thing is alfo attempted, in other inftances, by gloffes and ftrained interpretations. For example: Chrift is frequently faid in the Scriptures to have died *for* us: which we underftand to mean that he died *inftead of* us: and hence we argue, that his death was the direct and immediate occafion of our deliverance from death. And this, it muft be owned, is the obvious fenfe of the words. But the Socinian propofes another interpretation. For we are told that, in general, Chrift's dying *for us*, may be interpreted of his dying *on our account*, or *for our benefit*. " Or if," proceeds our Author, " when rigoroufly interpreted, it fhould be " found that if Chrift had not died, we muft
" have

" have died, it is ftill however only *confequen-*
" *tially* fo, and by no means *properly* and *di-*
" *rectly* fo, as a *fubftitute* for us. For if, in
" confequence of Chrift not having been fent
" to inftruct and reform the world, mankind
" had continued unreformed, and the necef-
" fary confequence of Chrift's coming was
" his death, by whatever means, and in
" whatever manner it was brought about, it
" is plain that there was, in fact, no other al-
" ternative, but his death, or ours. How
" natural then was it, efpecially to writers
" accuftomed to the ftrong figurative expref-
" fion of the Eaft, to fay that he died *in our*
" *ftead*, without meaning it in a ftrict and
" proper fenfe; as if God had abfolutely re-
" quired the death of Chrift, in order to fa-
" tisfy his juftice for our fins, and as a necef-
" fary means of his forgiving us [c]." And thus, while the words clearly afcribe a direct and immediate efficacy to the death of Chrift, which is alfo agreeable to the untortured fenfe of other paffages, the propofed interpretation labours to deftroy this efficacy, and to place the death of the Saviour upon a level with that of a mere Prophet, or Martyr: and, for

[c] Hift. of Cor. p. 199.

this

SERMON V.

thispurpofe, unwarrantably fubftitutes a remote and unnatural fenfe, in the room of the plain and obvious one, merely for the fake of accommodating the language of Scripture to the interpreter's preconceived opinions.

But I need not dwell upon inftances of this kind. For, unlefs it can be pofitively fhewn that the doctrine of Atonement makes no part of the fcheme of Chriftianity, but is foreign to the intention of the facred writers, all fuch paffages as apparently favour this doctrine, may juftly be cited in its fupport, notwithftanding they may, by a ftrained interpretation, be taken in another fenfe. Now that there are paffages which do thus apparently favour this doctrine, and cannot, without ftraining, be otherwife interpreted, will not be denied. It is acknowledged by our Adverfary himfelf; who having declared that the opinion, which he oppofes to this doctrine of Atonement, is the doctrine of reafon, and of the Old Teftament, and is likewife agreeable to the general tenor of the New Teftament, concludes his hiftory of this doctrine with this remarkable conceffion. " In this, then, let " us acquiefce, not doubting but that, *though* " *perhaps not at prefent*, we fhall in time be " able, without any effort or ftraining, to explain

"plain all particular expreſſions in the apoſ-
"tolical epiſtles, &c. in a manner perfectly
"conſiſtent with the general ſtrain of their
"own writings, and the reſt of the Scrip-
"tures [d]."

It appears, then, from the confeſſion of our Adverſary, that the language of Scripture is, on ſome occaſions at leaſt, undeniably for us; and that there are paſſages, the force of which can only be eluded, by wreſting the words from their natural and obvious ſenſe, and torturing them into a different meaning. But if this mode of proceeding be fair and allowable, there is no article of the Chriſtian faith which may not be called in queſtion. For the imperfection of language neceſſarily ſubjects the moſt preciſe and accurate expreſſions to miſconſtruction; and let a writer be ever ſo careful and guarded, the ingenuity of a ſophiſt will ſtill contrive to pervert his meaning, and to impoſe upon his words a ſenſe different from that which they obviouſly bear, and which he originally intended. And ſince the language of Scripture is no leſs capable of perverſion and miſconſtruction than that of any other book, it follows, that

[d] Hiſt. of Cor. p. 279.

neither

SERMON V.

neither the doctrine of Atonement, nor any other doctrine, can be so positively and clearly revealed, as wholly to preclude all possibility of dispute and opposition: so that the force of any language, even more precise and accurate, if such could be found, than that in which the doctrine is at present revealed, might, by the same means, be evaded, and the doctrine itself called in question.

But we should remember that God hath given us a revelation of his will, not to exercise our wit and ingenuity, but for our information and instruction. To the poor is the Gospel preached: and therefore, in all necessary points, its meaning cannot be dark and intricate, discoverable only by the wise and learned; but must be simple and intelligible, adapted to the capacity of those for whose use it was designed. A forced interpretation is always to be suspected: and even where the words of Scripture will, without effort or straining, admit of different senses, the preference should be given, where it is justly due, to the most natural and obvious. And though we grant in general, that, in order to preserve the consistency of Revelation, recourse must sometimes be had to a more remote, and perhaps a figurative sense; we may at least require that it be not done, but upon sufficient grounds, and where the necessity is most apparent. And we should be extremely careful, left affection for a favourite hypothesis influence our judgment; left, while, in support of this hypothesis, we labour to reconcile apparent discordances in the sacred volume, we in reality pervert its meaning, to the prejudice of some important article of our Christian faith.

The application of these reflections to the case before us, must in part have appeared already; and will hereafter more fully appear, when we come to consider the ground, upon which our Historian justifies that method of interpretation, which we have been examining in the preceding Discourse.

SERMON

SERMON VI.

1 Cor. i. 23.

We preach Chrift crucified; to the Jews a ftumbling-block, and to the Greeks foolifhnefs.

AN eftablifhed opinion, which claims to be a Chriftian doctrine, and to be derived from the Scriptures, cannot be oppofed with the leaft profpect of fuccefs, unlefs it can be fhewn, that the Advocates of this opinion have miftaken the meaning of the infpired writers, and have appealed in its behalf to paffages of Scripture, which may and ought to be taken in a different fenfe. This accordingly has been attempted by the Hiftorian of the Corruptions of Chriftianity; who contends, that the fcriptural reprefentations of the death of Chrift, and various ex-

SERMON VI.

preffions relating to it, which are commonly fuppofed to favour the doctrine of Atonement, have been greatly mifunderftood, and ought to be interpreted in another and a better manner, more confonant, as he conceives, with the general tenor of Revelation, and the true end of our Saviour's advent.

In order fully to eftablifh this pofition, it is plainly incumbent upon him to prove thefe two things: firft, that the words of Scripture are capable of another fenfe; and, fecondly, that this other fenfe ought, in the prefent inftance, to be admitted.

In the laft Difcourfe we confidered the general method of interpretation, by which he endeavours to prove the firft of thefe points; and found it to confift in torture and evafion, rather than in direct explanation; and in the arbitrary impofition of a remote and figurative fenfe, contrary to the obvious meaning of the expreffions themfelves, and the manifeft intention of the facred writers.

But, for argument's fake, let us fuppofe that he has thus far fucceeded: let us allow that the fenfe propofed, although forced and unnatural, is neverthelefs not wholly inadmiffible; but might be received, did the neceffity of the cafe require it. And let us now proceed

proceed to examine, whether such necessity really does exist; whether our Historian has proved the second thing required, and has made out such a case, as will justify our rejection of the plain and obvious meaning of the sacred writings, in order to substitute in its room that remote and figurative sense, for which he contends.

By referring to the History itself, it will be found, that our Opponent, before he ventures to propose his interpretation of the passages relating to our present subject, first prepares the way for its more easy admission, by attempting to prove, that the doctrine of Atonement makes no part of that scheme of religion which is delivered to us in the Scriptures, but is wholly of human invention. And indeed, could this be clearly and undeniably proved, I would no longer dispute against the proposed interpretation. For in that case the sacred writers could never have had it in contemplation to reveal this doctrine; and consequently their language, whatever might be its apparent meaning, must really bear a different sense; and any consistent sense, however remote, would be preferable to one, by which a mere human device is constituted a Christian

Christian doctrine. I am therefore by no means unwilling that the admiſſibility of the propoſed interpretation ſhould be made to depend upon the ſucceſs of this attempt. Let us therefore conſider the objections taken againſt our doctrine upon this ground, and examine the arguments, advanced by our Hiſtorian, in proof of the poſition above-mentioned, viz. that the doctrine of Atonement makes no part of that ſcheme of religion, which is contained in the Scriptures.

And, firſt, we are told, that " it is hardly
" poſſible not to ſuſpect the truth of this
" doctrine, when we conſider that the gene-
" ral maxims to which it may be reduced,
" are no where laid down, or aſſerted, in the
" Scriptures." And this, it is inſinuated, is contrary to the uſual practice of the ſacred writers, who generally " aſſign the reaſons of
" ſuch of the Divine proceedings reſpecting
" the human race, as are more difficult to be
" comprehended, and the neceſſity and pro-
" priety of which are not very obvious, and
" might be liable to be called in queſtion[a]."

That ſuch is the uſual practice of the ſacred

[a] Hiſt. of Cor. v. i. p. 154.

writers, is an affertion, of which no proof whatfoever is adduced. And I conceive that the principle itfelf, if it were once admitted as a proper rule of judging in Divine things, might be productive of much mifchief, and would tend to the overthrow of all religion, both natural and revealed. For upon this ground we fhould be at liberty to call in queftion every Divine proceeding, the reafon of which was not exprefsly affigned, or the neceffity and propriety of which we could not comprehend. Now, in the common and general courfe of things, it is allowed, that the ways of God are frequently dark and intricate; nor is it always eafy to reconcile them to our natural notions of Divine perfection. But fhall we on this account perverfely call in queftion the fuperintending providence, the wifdom, the juftice, or the goodnefs of the Deity? Rather let us confefs our own weaknefs and incapacity, and adore that depth which we cannot fathom. It is the fame in the cafe of Revelation; the general intention of which is to teach us *what* God wills, not *why* he wills it; and to acquaint us, not fo much with the reafons of his proceedings refpecting man, as with the proceedings themfelves: and he expects from us an humble acquiefcence,

quiefcence, although we may not readily comprehend the neceffity, or even the propriety, of the things revealed. It is fufficient for us to know, in general, that God never acts without a caufe, and that what he does is always wife and proper to be done.

Were it neceffary to prove the general doctrine here advanced, I might inftance, in confirmation of it, the law impofed upon the firft man; of which neither the end, nor the reafons, are, as far as I know, any where declared. We may indeed *infer*, that the end propofed was the trial of man's obedience. But why an efpecial trial was at all appointed, and why fuch a trial as that to which man was fubjected, we are not told. With refpect alfo to the influence of man's tranfgreffion, we are told, in general, that this one man's difobedience introduced fin and death into the world, and corrupted and depraved the whole human race. But why the influence fhould be thus extenfive; why the tranfgreffor fhould not alone fuffer, but fhould be permitted to tranfmit the ftain through a long feries of future generations; thefe are circumftances with which we are nearly concerned, but of which we are in total ignorance. In like manner we are told in general, that the

recovery

SERMON VI.

recovery of fallen man, and his restoration to the favour of God, was effected " through " the redemption that is in Jesus Christ; " whom God hath set forth to be a propitiation " through faith in his blood [b]:" but the reasons of this dispensation, why a propitiation should be ordained at all; and why such a propitiation as that which the Divine wisdom thought fit to adopt; and how the blood of Christ attained the end for which it was shed, are circumstances which, perhaps, are no where expressly revealed. But let the word of God still stand sure: and let us with becoming thankfulness still receive the dispensation itself, and not presumptuously reject it, because we are not admitted to the councils of heaven, and indulged with a knowledge of every circumstance connected with it. Notwithstanding, therefore, we may not be able to discover, in any of the books of Scripture, the principle upon which the doctrine of Atonement is founded, this need not excite in us any surprise, nor ought the doctrine itself to fall, upon this account, under the least suspicion.

[b] Rom. iii. 24, 25.

But

SERMON VI.

But let me not be thought to have miftaken the force of our Hiftorian's argument. I am aware that his intention was not to affert generally, that there is nothing laid down in the Scriptures which can be affumed as the principle, upon which the doctrine of Atonement is founded; but only, that the principle which the doctrine itfelf holds forth, or rather, that which fome affertors of the doctrine have affumed as its principle, is no where to be found in any of the books of Scripture. The principle here alluded to, upon which the modern doctrine of Atonement is reprefented entirely to depend, is the following, viz. that God cannot extend his mercy to finners, till his juftice has been fully fatisfied. It muft not be denied, that this principle may be collected and inferred from the writings of fome upon the fubject, who, in explaining and defending this doctrine, may, as we are here told, have afferted, that " fin is of
" fo heinous a nature, that God cannot par-
" don it without an adequate fatisfaction
" being made to his juftice, and to the ho-
" nour of his laws and government." But ftill I contend, that affertions of this kind are not necefarily falfe, becaufe they cannot be found in the holy Scriptures; nor, fecondly,
could

could they even be proved to be falfe, would the doctrine of Atonement be at all affected.

And, firft, let us fuppofe that the principle affigned is no where to be found in the holy Scriptures; ftill, I fay, it does not follow that it is not the true principle upon which the doctrine is founded. It has already been obferved, that the Scriptures do not always affign the reafons of the Divine proceedings. But fince God cannot be fuppofed ever to act without a caufe, whatever he does muft be founded upon fomething in his own nature, or in the nature and reafon of the thing, which makes it wife and proper to be done. Confequently where the Scriptures are filent refpecting the reafon of any of the Divine proceedings, there ftill muft be a reafon; and any affignable reafon may be the true one, which is not repugnant to the nature of God, or inconfiftent with the nature of the thing revealed. And therefore, in the prefent cafe, it does not immediately follow, that the principle affigned is not the true principle upon which the doctrine of Atonement is founded, notwithftanding we grant that it is no where laid down as fuch in any of the books of Scripture.

But, fecondly, let us further grant, that the filence

silence of the Scriptures is sufficient to impeach the principle of any doctrine; and consequently that the one here assigned, is not the true principle upon which the doctrine in question is founded: yet how does this affect the doctrine itself? If God does sometimes conceal from us the reasons of his proceedings, there may, and occasionally there will be cases, in which we must confess our ignorance, and be contented to rely implicitly upon the wisdom and goodness of the Deity for the rectitude and fitness of what he does, without presuming to reduce his measures to our own standard of what is right and fit. But, if the truth of a doctrine still remains sure and unimpaired, notwithstanding our ignorance of the foundation upon which it rests, and our consequent inability to fix it upon any principle at all, as little surely must it be affected by our error in fixing it upon a false principle.

I am led to insist the more strenuously upon this point, because many, if not the greater part, of the arguments commonly urged by Socinian writers, are directed against the doctrine considered under this view of it; viz. as maintaining the necessity of an *adequate*

quate satisfaction to the Divine justice, in order to the pardon of sin: and when, as they think, they have made it appear, that this opinion is not supported by any good authority, they immediately glory, as though they had obtained a complete victory. Whereas, in truth, arguments of this kind bear not at all upon the main question; which is, not why an atonement was ordained, or to which of the Divine attributes it was made; but simply, whether it has been made at all. So that the ground, which the enemy is thus eager to dispute, might be wholly abandoned, and fairly given up, without the least injury to our cause. Not that the ground is in itself altogether untenable. For arguments are by no means wanting, by which, were it necessary, we might sufficiently justify and defend the general position, that Christ died to make satisfaction for the sins of men: and still further, that this satisfaction was made to Divine justice. By the justice of God, we here mean that attribute of his nature, by which, in the impartial administration of his righteous government, he ordains the punishment of those who transgress his laws. For, agreeably to the practice of the sacred writers, in speaking of the Deity, we distinguish in

his

his nature various attributes, obtained by analogy from corresponding attributes in our own; to which we are wont to refer the Divine proceedings, each to that attribute which is peculiarly adapted to it. Thus the creation of the univerfe we attribute to his power; its harmony and order, to his wifdom; the bountiful provifion made for our prefervation and fupport, to his goodnefs; the favour fhewn to penitent finners, to his mercy; and in like manner the punifhment of obftinate tranfgreffors, to his juftice. Now it is agreeable to the natural apprehenfions of our own mind, that God, who is effentially pure and holy, and who neceffarily holds fin in abhorrence, fhould be offended with thofe who wilfully tranfgrefs his laws; and they, with whom he is offended, may reafonably expect from his juftice the due reward of their evil deeds. Declarations to the fame effect abound in the holy Scriptures; from which we further learn, that the Divine difpleafure againft fin was not appeafed without a propitiation. It is therefore reafonable to conclude that it was, on fome account or other, wife and proper that he fhould he propitiated, before he pardoned fin. And fince, in confequence of the pardon thus obtained, his juftice no longer required

required that the punishment due to sin should be inflicted upon the offenders; is not this in effect to say, that, by means of the appointed propitiation for sin, satisfaction was made to the Divine justice. Though, therefore, I would not limit the Divine power, and say what the Almighty Governor of the universe can, or cannot do, in his own world, and with his own creatures; though I would not assert, that an *adequate* satisfaction to Divine justice, or indeed any satisfaction at all, was absolutely and indispensably necessary to the pardon of sin (for of this, independently of Revelation, we can know nothing in our present state); yet I scruple not to say, in general terms, that, by the appointment of God, satisfaction has been made to his justice, and that without such satisfaction he did not think fit to remit the punishment of sin. What would have ensued, supposing no satisfaction had been appointed; whether in such case it would have been consistent with the nature and attributes of God, that he should be propitious to fallen man; is a question concerning which the Scriptures are totally silent, and therefore we presume not to determine.

And thus the notion of a satisfaction, although no where, as far as I know, expressly asserted

aſſerted in the Scriptures, appears neverthelefs to be agreeable to our own apprehenſions of the Divine nature, and to the account given in the Scriptures of the Divine proceedings; and may therefore ſafely be admitted. If, after all, our Adverſaries ſtill remain hoſtile to this mode of expreſſing our opinion, I wiſh not to conteſt the matter; becauſe, as I before obſerved, it is a conteſt in which the merits of the queſtion are not at all concerned. We have done all that can reaſonably be required of us, when we have proved from the Scriptures, that Chriſt, by dying for us, became the propitiation for our ſins: nor is it in the leaſt neceſſary that we ſhould further ſhew, what were the reaſons which moved God to ordain ſuch a propitiation, or by what mode of operation the death of Chriſt effects the purpoſe for which it was ordained.

But the objection does not ſtop here. For we are told, not only that the ſacred writers, in ſpeaking of the malignant nature of ſin, never aſſert, that God cannot pardon it without an adequate ſatisfaction being made to his juſtice; but further, that " the contrary " ſentiment occurs every where; viz. that " repentance and a good life are, *of them-*
" ſelves,

" *selves*, sufficient to recommend us to the
" Divine favour [c]." This part of the objection directly meets the question; and, if it could be supported, would overthrow, not only the notion of a satisfaction to Divine justice, but also the whole doctrine of Atonement, with every modification of it. For if repentance and a good life are, either in their own nature, or by the express appointment of God, sufficient *of themselves* to recommend us to the Divine favour, then the propitiation for which we contend, must be altogether unnecessary, and therefore would not have been appointed. Here then we may be fairly said to be at issue; and upon the determination of this point, the decision of the controversy may be made to depend. Now, that repentance and a good life are pleasing in the sight of God, and will be rewarded with his favourable acceptance, the Scriptures unquestionably declare, and we most thankfully acknowledge. This, therefore, makes no part of the present question; which refers solely to this circumstance, *how,* or *on what account,* repentance and a good life came to be thus acceptable to God? whether they are so *of*

[c] Hist. of Cor. p. 155.

themselves;

themselves; that is, on account of their own intrinsic value, without reference to any atonement or propitiation for sin; or whether they are become so, through the atonement made by Jesus Christ? The expressions, and passages of Scripture, which apparently favour our side of the question, are, notwithstanding any insinuation to the contrary, neither few nor obscure [d]; and therefore, before we agree to let go our faith, and suffer these passages to be explained away, it behoves us carefully to enquire, whether our Opponent has fully and satisfactorily made good his assertion, that repentance and a good life are declared in the Scriptures to be, *of themselves*, sufficient to recommend us to the Divine favour. Where then, let us ask, is any such declaration to be found? Is it in the addresses made by inspired persons to notorious sinners, and in the general exhortations to repentance? We are indeed referred to these; and it is insinuated that they are so expressed, as to exclude the doctrine for which we contend. For we are told, that, " notwithstanding so many no-
" torious sinners, particular persons, and
" whole nations, are addressed by inspired

[d] Hist. of Cor. p. 156.

" persons,

" perſons, and their conduct ſtrongly remon-
" ſtrated againſt in the courſe of the ſacred
" hiſtory, none of them are ever directed. to
" any thing further than their own hearts and
" lives. *Return unto me, and I will return
" unto you*, is the ſubſtance of all they ſay on
" theſe occaſions [e]."

Now had the queſtion been concerning the *acceptableneſs* of repentance, ſuch paſſages, as contain general declarations of God's willingneſs to receive returning ſinners, would have been urged with propriety and effect. But concerning this there is no diſpute. We all agree that God will be merciful to ſuch as truly repent, and turn to him; and therefore we freely acknowledge all that paſſages of this kind can be ſaid to prove; which is ſimply, that repentance and a good life are acceptable to God; but by no means that they are *of themſelves* acceptable. And therefore in vain are we referred to theſe addreſſes and exhortations, for ſentiments incompatible with the doctrine of Atonement.

If it be inſiſted, that although paſſages of this kind do not poſitively prove that repentance and a good life are of themſelves accept-

[e] Hiſt. of Cor. p. 156.

able, yet they afford a kind of prefumptive proof againſt the doctrine of Atonement; becauſe, allowing it to be true, it is reaſonable to conclude, that frequent intimations of it would have accompanied the exhortations to repentance, and the declarations of Divine mercy, which every where abound in the ſacred books; I wiſh it to be confidered, on the other hand, that theſe exhortations and declarations are all of them ſubſequent to the promiſe of a Redeemer: for, according to our doctrine, the covenant of works was immediately ſucceeded by the covenant of grace; and even from the fall of Adam, God became propitious to mankind, in conſequence of the atonement to be made in after times, and, in the contemplation of the Divine mind, confidered as already made, by Jeſus Chriſt; who on this account is called " the Lamb, ſlain " from the foundation of the world ꞌ." So that the addreſſes to ſinners, and the exhortations to repentance, which abound in the Scriptures, are founded upon, and conſequently preſuppoſe, this work of Chriſt: and therefore are not to be confidered as declarations of the terms upon which God, offended

ꞌ Rev. xiii. 8.

by

by the sins of men, will be appeased, and become propitious; for he who is so merciful as to declare his acceptance of sincere repentance, in the room of that sinless perfection which was required by the first covenant, must be considered as already propitiated; but are rather expressions of his compassionate concern for his creatures, and persuasions that they would not, by their own obstinacy and wilful disobedience, deprive themselves of those blessings, which, now that he is reconciled, he is willing to bestow upon them. It would therefore be no impeachment of our doctrine, even if it could be proved that these addresses and exhortations, which thus imply, and are founded upon, a previous reconciliation, are not constantly, or indeed commonly, accompanied by express assertions of the reconciliation itself. Indeed such assertions are hardly to be expected any where in the Old Testament, under which both the reconciliation, and the manner of it, were but darkly intimated in promises and predictions, and faintly represented by types and ceremonial observances: and in any part of Scripture are rather to be sought in such passages, as expressly treat of man's fall, and the method by which he was restored to a state of grace and falvation, than in thofe which prefuppofe this ftate of falvation, and are addreffed to fuch as have already been called to it, and are actually in it.

We fhould, therefore, be little difpofed to allow that repentance and a good life are *of themfelves* fufficient to recommend us to the Divine favour, even if it could be fhewn, that the facred writers in general, and efpecially thofe of the Old Teftament, do not, in their addreffes and exhortations to finners, make mention of the doctrine for which we contend. If, indeed, the intention of our doctrine had been to fuperfede repentance and a good life, the argument of our Opponent would not have been without force. But this is not the cafe. A propitiation for fin, and the acceptablenefs of repentance in confequence of that propitiation, are perfectly confiftent; and, for aught that we know, are infeparably connected. We know not whether, without a propitiation, repentance would have been acceptable to God, or even poffible to man: at leaft it is not for us to feparate what God hath joined together. And yet upon their feparation the opinion of our Adverfary, that repentance and a good life are *of themfelves* fufficient to recommend us to
the

the Divine favour, entirely depends. For this opinion is virtually founded upon the two following affumptions: firft, that there is nothing in the nature or attributes of God, which requires a propitiation for fin, in order to make repentance acceptable; for if there be, then repentance and a good life are not of themfelves fufficient: fecondly, that if there had been no propitiation, repentance and a good life would, notwithftanding, have been poffible to man.

And, firft, the opinion, that repentance and a good life are of themfelves fufficient, is founded upon the affumption that there is nothing in the Divine nature, or attributes, which requires a propitiation for fin; an affumption, incapable, as I conceive, of the leaft proof. For the pofition itfelf prefuppofes fuch an intimate knowledge of the Deity, as is not attainable by man in his prefent ftate. "Canft thou by fearching find out "God? Canft thou find out the Almighty "unto perfection? It is as high as heaven, "what canft thou do? deeper than hell, "what canft thou know [g]?" It is referved for us in a future ftate, to fee God as he is.

[g] Job xi. 7, 8.

At

SERMON VI.

At present our faculties are limited, and able to give us a very imperfect knowledge even of the things which are before us; and can by no means raise us to the knowledge of him who is infinite and invisible. We know not God as he is; and therefore, unassisted by revelation, we cannot determine what his attributes do, or do not, require. Of this we may be assured, that he best knows what is agreeable to the purity of his own nature, and what will preserve the glory of his attributes undiminished and unimpeached. Instead, therefore, of leaning to our own understandings, and of previously determining that nothing relating to God can be true, which does not approve itself to our fallible judgment, it will be safer far to take his word for our guide, and to receive with humility and submission whatever we find to be there revealed; in the fullest confidence that his proceedings, however they may appear to us, must, in themselves, be wise and good.

The other assumption, that repentance and a good life would have been possible to man, if no propitiation had been made, is equally incapable of proof. If, as we believe, a propitiation has been made, it is impossible for us to say what, without a propitiation, would have

have been our state. We know not the full and precise meaning of the Divine threat, "thou shalt surely die[h]:" whether it was intended to convey to man, that, upon the commission of sin, he should immediately and at once be deprived of being, and reduced to his primitive nothing; or only that he, who was originally designed for a life of immortality and incorruption, should become mortal, and subject to death. But, whatever be the meaning of the words, this at least is certain, that the provision which the promise of a Saviour made for the expiation of man's offence, reversed, in some measure, the sentence of condemnation which the law denounced, and placed the transgressor in a state far different from that in which he would have been, had the vengeance of God been fully executed. It was this gracious promise which made man again an object of favour; which again placed him in a state of trial; and again brought within his reach life and immortality. And therefore to the appointment of Jesus Christ to be a propitiation, we owe that God vouchsafes to accept that repentance, and that imperfect virtue, of which man in his present

[h] Gen. ii. 17.

state is capable. And who will say, that the very ability to repent, and the very existence of that virtue, imperfect as it is, must not be ascribed to the same cause? Let us consider the case of offenders, whose rank in the scale of being was once higher than that of man, even at his first creation : I mean the angels who kept not their first estate. By their fall, they were lost for ever; being, as St. Jude expresses it, " reserved in everlasting chains " under darkness unto the judgment of the " great day [1]," without the most distant hope of escaping that fiery indignation, which shall devour the adversaries of God. In their case repentance would be unavailable. But we no where read that they either do or can repent. Instead of that meek contrition, that godly sorrow, which worketh repentance unto salvation, and inspires an humble hope of pardon and acceptance; theirs is a frantic grief, arising from disappointed pride, and venting itself in an impious and malicious rage against that unerring justice, which has unalterably fixed their doom. It is not for us to say, why that grace, which was vouchsafed to man, was denied to them. We know only

[1] Jude 6.

that

that for them no propitiation was appointed; and who can tell what, without a propitiation, would have been the state of fallen man? Perhaps altogether as hopeless and deplorable as the state of fallen angels! We, like them, might have been objects, not of mercy, but of vengeance; for ever cut off from God, and doomed to irrevocable condemnation! At all events the contrary cannot be proved; and proved it ought to be, before we admit that repentance and a good life are, *of themselves*, sufficient to recommend us to the Divine favour.

But it is contended, that the Scriptures themselves favour this opinion, since they " uniformly represent God as our universal " parent, pardoning sinners *freely*; that is," we are told, " from his natural goodness and " mercy, whenever they truly repent, and " reform their lives [k]." And this representation of the Divine being, it is further contended, is inconsistent with the doctrine of Atonement; which, by making the pardon of sin to depend upon a foreign consideration, is supposed to limit and impose a restraint

[k] Hist. of Cor. p. 156.

upon that goodnefs and compaffion, which the Scriptures affirm to be free and unconfined.

It will not be difficult to fhew, that this objection, if allowed to be valid, would militate no lefs againſt the opinion of our Adverfary, than againſt the doctrine of Atonement: but that in reality it proceeds upon a grofs miſtake both of the true fenfe of Scripture, and of the nature of our doctrine. But becaufe it is an objection which has been frequently urged, and upon which our Adverfaries feem to depend with no little confidence, it will be proper to enter more at large into the fubject, than can conveniently be done upon the prefent occafion: I fhall therefore referve the full confideration of it for the next Difcourfe.

SERMON

SERMON VII.

1 Cor. i. 23.

We preach Chrift crucified; to the Jews a ftumbling-block, and to the Greeks foolifh-nefs.

AMONG the various objections, which have been urged by Socinian writers againft the doctrine of Atonement, none has been repeated more frequently, or preffed with greater earneftnefs and confidence, than that which I am now to confider: I mean, the fuppofed inconfiftency of this doctrine, with the free grace and goodnefs of God. At the fame time there is no objection which refts upon a weaker foundation, or betrays a more grofs mifunderftanding of the doctrine, which it profeffes to oppofe.

The Hiftorian of the Corruptions of Chriftianity ftates and fupports this objection in the following manner. Having afferted, agreeably to the quotation made at the clofe of the laſt Difcourfe, that the Scriptures " uniformly reprefent God as our univerfal " parent, pardoning finners *freely*, that is, " from his natural goodnefs and mercy, when- " ever they truly repent and reform their " lives," he thus proceeds : " All the decla- " rations of Divine mercy are made without " referve or limitation to the truly penitent; " through all the books of Scripture, with- " out the moft diftant hint of any regard " being had to the fufferings or merit of any " being whatever." In proof of this pofition, he brings from the Old Teftament the declaration which God made of his character to Mofes, prefently after the Ifraelites had finned, in making the golden calf. " And the " Lord paffed by before him, and proclaimed " the Lord, the Lord God, merciful and gra- " cious, long fuffering, abundant in goodnefs " and truth, keeping mercy for thoufands, " forgiving iniquity, and tranfgreffion, and " fin [a]." And then, as a further proof,

[a] Exod. xxxiv. 6, 7.

upon

upon which he seems chiefly to depend, he quotes from the New Testament the declaration of the Apostle, that we are *justified freely by the grace of God*[b]. " Now certainly," proceeds he, " if the favour had been pro-
" cured by the suffering of another person,
" it could not have been said to be bestowed
" *freely*[c]." And again in another place, commenting upon these same words, he observes, that the word *freely* " implies that forgive-
" ness is the *free gift* of God, and proceeds
" from his essential goodness and mercy, with-
" out regard to any foreign consideration
" whatever."

Let me briefly bring to your recollection, that the principal position, mentioned in the preceding passage, is the following; viz. that the declarations of Divine mercy are made without reserve or limitation to the truly penitent, without the most distant hint of any regard being had to the sufferings or merit of any being whatever. Now that God hath declared in Scripture, that sincere penitents are the objects of his mercy, I readily admit. But then I contend, that this very circum-

[b] Rom. iii. 24.—Tit. iii. 7.
[c] Hist. of Cor. vol. i. p. 156.

stance implies a reserve and limitation. Under the Gospel-dispensation, offers of mercy are made, not to the penitent merely, but to all without exception. Our Lord commanded his Apostles to " preach the Gos-" pel to every creature ᵉ." And he says of himself, that he " came to call *sinners* to re-" pentance ᶠ." But of these such only as obey the call, are accepted of God. Since, then, forgiveness is not extended indiscriminately to all who have sinned, but is confined to such sinners, as by repentance are qualified for so great a blessing, there is, unquestionably, in the mode of God's dispensing mercy, a reserve and limitation.

As for the other assertion, that there is not in any of the books of Scripture the most distant hint that God, in dispensing mercy, pays regard to the sufferings or merit of any being whatever, it may be opposed by a multitude of instances to the contrary, collected from various parts of Scripture. The Psalmist, speaking of the wonders which God had wrought for the deliverance of his people out of Egypt, and for their preservation in the wilderness, declares, that these mercies were

---

ᵉ Mark xvi. 15. ᶠ Mark ii. 17.

vouchsafed

SERMON VII.

vouchsafed unto them, because God "re-
"membered his holy promise, and Abraham
"his servant [g]." And when the Israelites
had provoked God by their sin, in making the
golden calf, Moses, in interceding for them,
does not recommend them to mercy on account of their sincere repentance (for at this
very time they were engaged in the idolatrous
act), but he urges a foreign consideration;
namely, the promise which God had made to
their forefathers, his tried and faithful servants: "Remember," says he, "Abraham,
"Isaac, and Israel, thy servants, to whom
"thou swarest by thine own self, and saidst
"unto them, I will multiply your seed as the
"stars of heaven, and all this land that I
"have spoken of, will I give unto your seed,
"and they shall inherit it for ever." And
his prayer was heard; for we read that " the
"Lord repented of the evil which he thought
"to do unto his people [h]." And in another
place Moses petitions for them, not on account of their repentance, or obedience, for
he acknowledges their obstinacy and disobedience; but on account of himself, and in
consideration of the favour which he had him-

[g] Pf. cv. 42.   [h] Exod. xxxii. 13, 14.

self found with God. "If now," says he, "I have found grace in thy sight, O Lord, "let my Lord, I pray thee, go amongst us "(for it is a stiff-necked people), and pardon "our iniquity and our sin, and take us for "thine inheritance." And God granted his petition; for in the very next verse he declares, that he made a covenant with them [j]. And in after-times the idolatry of King Solomon was not punished, as it deserved, with the loss of his kingdom; but God was pleased to continue him king all the days of his life, for David his father's sake; " because," says a prophet speaking in the name of God, " he "kept my commandments and my statutes[k]." And again in the reign of Hezekiah, when the Assyrians came up against Jerusalem, God declares by the prophet Isaiah, " I will defend "this city to save it for mine own sake, and "for my servant David's sake [l]." So that if, upon this subject, we are allowed to have recourse to the Old Testament, there is, not a distant hint, but positive proof, that God does not always dispense mercy to the truly penitent, merely as such, but sometimes pays

[j] Exod. xxxiv. 9, 10.
[l] Is. xxxvii. 35.
[k] 1 Kings xi. 34.

regard

regard to a foreign confideration; by which he is even moved to be favourable to thofe who continue ftill in their fins.

Nor is our doctrine in the leaft invalidated, or the opinion of our Adverfary at all confirmed, by the paffage quoted from the Old Teftament, which, at moft, is only filent refpecting a circumftance not neceffary to be mentioned. For God is here merely proclaiming his name and his attributes, in compliance with the requeft of his fervant Mofes, who had defired to fee his glory: but profeffes not to declare either the reafons of his gracious dealings with mankind, or the method by which he thinks fit to carry his benevolent defigns into effect. And therefore in vain was this paffage adduced to prove, that God, in fhewing mercy, pays no regard to the fufferings or merit of any being whatever.

Still lefs to our Adverfary's purpofe is the paffage from the New Teftament, which, even in the fenfe impofed upon it by himfelf, will be found, upon examination, no more to prove his principal pofition, than the former quotation from the Old Teftament; and, in its true fenfe, is fo far from being conclufive againft us, that it is rather on our fide. " Being juftified," fays the Apoftle, " freely " by

" by his grace :" *freely*; that is, says our Author, " from the essential goodness and mercy " of God, without regard to any foreign con- " sideration whatever." And, taking the word in this sense, he argues, that, if " the " favour had been procured by the suffering " of another person, it could not have been " said to be bestowed freely." Now, upon the ground here assumed, a thing can then only be said to be done freely, when it is done unconditionally; when the will of the agent is unconfined, and exempt from the operation of any consideration without itself. But if this be the meaning of the term; if God, in the pardon of sin, be supposed to proceed after this method; then, to use the words of an eminent Prelate [m], the highest Antinomianism is the truest doctrine. For since forgiveness can only be accounted a free gift by being dependant upon no condition, and subject to no restriction, it follows, that the repentance and amendment of the offender himself are no more to be regarded, than the sufferings or merit of any other being; and consequently that all sinners, without reserve or limitation,

---

[m] Stillingfleet, in his Discourse concerning the true reason of the sufferings of Christ.

have

have an equal claim to pardon, whether they repent or no. If, to avoid so shocking a consequence, it be said that God is free to chuse the objects to whom he will shew mercy, and to impose upon them such restrictions, and to require in them such qualifications as he thinks fit; I contend it may, with equal reason, be asserted, that he is also free to dispense this mercy for such reasons, and by such methods, as he in his wisdom shall determine to be most conducive to his own glory, and the good of his creatures. And I know of no reason why a regard to the sufferings or merit of another person should any more destroy the freedom of the gift, than the requisition of certain qualifications in the object himself. And thus, upon the ground assumed by our Adversary, the argument, derived from this passage, either proves as much against him as against us, or, which is rather the case, proves nothing against either; and is therefore wholly inapplicable to the point in question.

But the argument itself proceeds upon a mistake of the Apostle's meaning. For the expression *freely*, has an immediate reference to ourselves, and to our own exertions in the work of justification, not to any thing which has been done by another in our behalf; and is here ufed to denote the manner in which the bleffing is beftowed, not the means by which it was procured. " Being juftified " freely by his grace:" freely; in the original δωρεαν; in the way of a gift, unmerited by us; and not in the way of a reward for our worthinefs or defert: agreeably to the affertion of the Apoftle in another place, " Not by works of righteoufnefs, which we " have done, but according to his mercy he " faved us ª." To be *juftified*, is to be accounted righteous in the fight of God, and to be admitted as fuch to his favour and acceptance. But man, in his fallen ftate, had nothing in himfelf, and could do nothing of himfelf, by which he might merit, or claim as his due, fo great a benefit. By fin he was become guilty before God, and fubject to the curfe of the law: by fin he had corrupted his faculties, and had loft much of that light and ftrength by means of which, while in a ftate of innocence, he had both a knowledge of his duty, and alfo ability to perform it: fo that unfinning obedience, which, under the firft covenant, was the duty of man, and which

ª Tit. iii. 5.

alone

SERMON VII.

alone could give him a right and title to life and happiness, was now no longer in his power. Having, therefore, no pretension to real righteousness, our absolution from the guilt of sin, and our admission to the character and privileges of righteous persons, must be imputed, not to our merit, but to God's grace; it is an act of mercy, which we must acknowledge and receive as a free gift, and not demand as a due reward.

Nor is the freedom of the gift destroyed, either by the conditions upon which it is bestowed, or by the means through which it was procured. Man being endued, under the first covenant, with powers fully adequate to the performance of an entire obedience, such an obedience might with justice be required of him; and being required, became his duty. And when, by the voluntary abuse of his faculties, he had lost the ability to perform his duty, this could impose no obligation upon God to accept of less. And therefore that God should cancel the first, and enter into a new covenant with us, in which he requires a duty better adapted to the natural powers still remaining to us, and hath moreover promised supernatural assistance in the performance of it; that instead of unsinning obedience,

dience, which, according to the tenor of the firſt covenant, he might ſtill have required, he ſhould accept of our ſincere endeavours to obey his will, and ſhould engage to abſolve from guilt, and to receive as righteous, all who truly repent and turn to him; this is throughout a proceeding, not of juſtice, but of mercy; and muſt be wholly afcribed, not to our merit, but to God's free grace. Notwithſtanding, therefore, repentance and good works are required under the new covenant, it is ſtill a covenant of *grace*; and the benefits of this covenant muſt ſtill be accounted a *gift*, the freedom of which is not deſtroyed, or in the leaſt diminiſhed, by the reſtriction under which it is offered.

Nor do the means, by which our juſtification was effected, in any reſpect alter its nature as a gift, or in the leaſt diminiſh its freedom. What theſe means are, the Apoſtle declares in the words immediately following; " Being juſtified freely by his grace, *through* " *the redemption that is in Jeſus Chriſt*:" and what we are to underſtand by this *redemption*, he tells us in another place; where, ſpeaking of Chriſt, he aſſures us, that in him " we " have redemption through his blood, *the for-*
" *givenefs*

"*givenefs of fins* [o]." Under the Gofpel-difpenfation, as under the Legal, a fhedding of blood was appointed in order to remiffion; and this blood was no other than that of Chrift himfelf; which, as the Prieft of his Church, he offered to God, and thus made an atonement for us, and procured that abfolution from the guilt of fin, without which we could not have been *juftified*, or accepted and treated as righteous perfons. And hence it is that we are faid to be " juftified through the re" demption that is in Jefus Chrift." But this redemption was not procured by us, or provided at our expence. It was the refult of the pure love of God; who, compaffionating our mifery, himfelf provided the means of our deliverance. And for this caufe he fent into the world his only-begotten fon, who voluntarily fubmitted to die upon the crofs, that he might become the propitiation for our fins, and reconcile us to God. Thus is the whole an entire act of mercy on the part of God and Chrift; begun and completed for our benefit, but without our intervention: and therefore, with refpect to us, the pardon of fin, and our confequent juftification, muft ftill be ac-

[o] Eph. i. 7.

counted a gift, notwithſtanding it comes to us " through the redemption that is in Jeſus " Chriſt."

And thus the doctrine of Atonement is ſo far from infringing, that it rather illuſtrates and diſplays the free grace and goodneſs of God: conſequently the objection which we have now been conſidering, not only will not bear the great ſtreſs which has been laid upon it, but is even wholly unfounded, and falls entirely to the ground.

The foregoing objection proceeds upon the ſuppoſition that the doctrine of Atonement is inconſiſtent with the poſitive declarations of Scripture. There are other objections, which are rather of a negative kind: being founded upon the entire omiſſion of this doctrine in the Old Teſtament; and upon the profound ſilence, obſerved in the New by our Lord and his Apoſtles, upon occaſions which apparently required them to treat of it with the greateſt openneſs and freedom.

And, in the firſt place, with reſpect to the Old Teſtament it is aſſerted, that, " if the " doctrine of Atonement be true, it cannot, " however, be pretended that David, or any " other pious perſon" mentioned in that
book,

book, " was at all acquainted with it." And from this pofition it is inferred, either that " the belief of this doctrine cannot be necef- " fary to falvation, or indeed of much confe- " quence :" or, fecondly, admitting the importance of the doctrine, that " the whole of " the Old Teftament is, throughout, a moft " unaccountable book, and the religion it " exhibits, defective in the moft effential ar- " ticle ᴾ." Now the truth of the pofition itfelf may juftly be called in queftion. For the Old Teftament contains many indubitable notices of this doctrine. A Saviour to come was exprefsly promifed, and plainly foretold : and the method of the falvation was fignified and reprefented by the inftitutions and ceremonial obfervances of the law. Though, therefore, the holy men of old had not that clear light which we under the Gofpel enjoy, they were not wholly in the dark : they, doubtlefs, many of them, faw enough to convince them that their carnal ordinances had a fpiritual meaning, and were not utterly unable to look through the fign to the thing fignified by it.

But even admitting that the pious perfons,

ᴾ Hift. of Cor. v. i. p. 157, 158.

mentioned

mentioned in the Old Testament, were wholly unacquainted with this doctrine, still we must not hastily infer, either that the doctrine is unnecessary, or that the Old Testament is defective. And first, it does not follow that the doctrine is unnecessary. We know that the revelation of Divine truth was not full and entire at once: its dawnings, in early times, were faint and obscure: as the world advanced, it gradually grew more clear and distinct; till at length it burst forth into a perfect day, at the appearance of him who is emphatically called *the light of the world*[q]. Now if the revelation of the Divine will has been thus gradual; if, under the Old Testament, it was only begun, and was not completed but by the preaching of Christ and his inspired Apostles; then must they, who lived before the times of the Gospel, of necessity have been unacquainted with many important truths. But let us not absurdly suppose that their ignorance can be any excuse for our unbelief, or, because a doctrine could not be believed before it was revealed, that therefore the belief of it, when revealed, is a matter of little consequence.

[q] John viii. 12.

Let

SERMON VII.

Let us attend to the force of this argument, when applied to that doctrine which, in the estimation of our Opponent, is of the greatest importance, as being the distinguishing doctrine of Christianity; I mean a resurrection to immortal life. Now it is most certain that this doctrine was not fully revealed before the coming of Christ. This our Opponent in effect acknowledges, when he asserts, that " the true and proper design of the Gospel, " and consequently of the preaching and of " the death of Christ, was to ascertain and " exemplify the great doctrines of a resurrec-" tion and of a future state ʳ." And indeed it would be difficult, perhaps it is impossible to produce from the Old Testament any passage, in which these doctrines are explicitly and undeniably asserted. And therefore, if known at all, of which some have doubted, they must have been very imperfectly known to the holy men of old. But if their ignorance does not lessen the importance of these doctrines, (and what Christian will contend that it does?) surely it cannot more affect the doctrine of Atonement; the belief of which, even allowing it to have been un-

ʳ Hist. of Cor. p. 175.

known

known to the antient people of God, is not, on this account, a matter of little confequence, or become in any refpect the lefs neceffary to falvation.

After what has been already faid, few words will fuffice to fhew the weaknefs of the other inference, viz. that, admitting the truth and importance of this doctrine, " the whole of " the Old Teftament is, throughout, a moft " unaccountable book, and the religion it ex- " hibits is defective in the moft effential ar- " ticle." For the very circumftance which, in the opinion of this Author, renders the Old Teftament a moft unaccountable book, is the neceffary confequence of the method by which the will of God has been revealed to mankind. It is not for us to enquire, why God concealed from one age of the world, what he afterwards thought fit to make known. Doubtlefs each diftinct revelation was adequate to the purpofe for which it was given, and is therefore perfect in its kind. At all events the omiffion, or imperfect revelation, of the doctrine of Atonement, can no more be called a defect in the Old Teftament, than the omiffion, or imperfect revelation, of a refurrection and a future ftate. And we pioufly believe that the ignorance of the antient

SERMON VII.

tient Israelites, respecting either doctrine, will be no hindrance to their enjoying the benefit of both: that in Christ Jesus, and in consequence of what he hath done, and suffered for mankind, their bodies will, with ours, be raised at the last day; and that such among them as, agreeably to the light afforded them, sincerely endeavoured to serve God, and to work righteousness, will be accepted of him.

But it is further objected, that " the Jews, " in our Saviour's time, had no idea of this " doctrine; for if they had, they would have " expected a suffering, and not a triumphant " Messiah [s]." And that their ignorance was not owing to any mistake respecting the character of the Messiah, and the true end of his coming into the world, is presently after attempted to be proved from the silence of our Saviour; who never, in the course of his preaching, pointed out to them their error, or drew their attention to the supposed great and only true cause of his death [t].

This argument of our Opponent, like the former, may fairly be turned upon himself; against whom it proves at least as much as

[s] Hist. of Cor. p. 158.   [t] Ibid. p. 159.

against us. The Jews, we are told, in our Saviour's time, had no idea that Messiah was to die for the sins of the world. But had they any more an idea that the true and proper end of his mission and death was "to "exemplify and ascertain the doctrines of a "resurrection and a future state?" It will not be pretended. One great and powerful sect among them disowned the very notion of a resurrection; and they all agreed in ascribing for Messiah's appearance a very different cause. They expected from his conquering arm the subjugation of their temporal enemies, and the possession of earthly power and grandeur. Even his own Disciples had no other expectation from him. Hence the rebuke of Peter, when he spake of the cruel mockings, and the ignominious death, which he was to accomplish at Jerusalem. "Be it "far from thee, Lord; this shall not be unto "thee[u]:" as if he thought it unbecoming the great Redeemer of God's people to submit to such indignity. And afterwards, having seen him, agreeably to his own predictions, betrayed and put to death, they seem to have given up all hope and expectation

[u] Matt. xvi. 22.

from him. " We trusted," say they, we once fondly hoped " that it had been he " which should have redeemed Israel ʷ." And so deeply rooted was this prejudice of theirs in expecting a triumphant, and not a suffering Messiah, that our Lord on this account accuses them of folly, and slowness of heart to believe what the prophets had spoken. " Ought not," says he, " Christ " to have suffered these things, and to enter " into his glory ˣ ?" As to the doctrine of a resurrection, they had not the least conception that it was at all connected with his mission and death. For, notwithstanding he concludes the account of his sufferings and crucifixion with an assurance that the third day he should rise again, the Evangelist tells us, that " they understood none of these " things: and this saying was hid from them, " neither knew they the things which were " spoken ʸ." And again, when, immediately after his transfiguration, he charged Peter, and James, and John, to tell no man what they had seen in the mount, till the son of man were risen from the dead; " they

ʷ Luke xxiv. 21.   ˣ Luke. xxiv. 25, 26.
ʸ Luke xviii. 34.

O 2   " kept,"

" kept," fays St. Mark, " that faying with
" themfelves, queftioning one with another
" what the rifing from the dead fhould
" mean [z]." And, fo far were they from expecting that fuch an event would happen, in
confequence of the predictions of the prophets, that, even after it had taken place,
St. John tells us, " as yet they knew not
" the Scripture, that he muft rife again from
" the dead [a]." And after they were fully
convinced of the reality of this event, they
were fo far from confidering his refurrection
as a pledge and a proof of their own, that they
thought it merely preparatory to his appearing in what they efteemed his proper character ; " Lord," fay they, " wilt thou at this
" time reftore again the kingdom to Ifrael[b]?"
But, notwithftanding, in thus expecting a triumphant Meffiah and a temporal Deliverer,
they had unqueftionably miftaken Meffiah's
character, and were wholly ignorant of what
our Hiftorian efteems the only true end of his
miffion, our Lord no where reproves them for
their error, or fets them right in a matter of
fo great importance. To his own Difciples
he fays nothing of his fufferings, till after

[z] Mark ix. 10.   [a] John xx. 9.   [b] Acts i. 6.

they

SERMON VII.

they had owned him to be the Christ[c]. Even after his resurrection, when they enquired of him, whether he would at that time accomplish what they still erroneously imagined to be the sole end of Messiah's appearance, he does not yet undeceive them: he eludes the question, by saying, " It is not for you to know the times or the seasons which the Father hath put in his own power[d]," promising them at the same time the gift of the Holy Ghost, who, by his Divine agency, should fully illuminate their understandings, and lead them into all truth. It appears, then, that this objection, if allowed to be valid against our doctrine, would be no less fatal to the opinion of our Adversary: for the Jews in general, and our Lord's Disciples among the rest, were as ignorant of the latter as of the former; and were suffered to continue in ignorance till the time came for the full discovery of the things pertaining to the kingdom of God.

But we are told that our Lord not only does not rectify the mistake of the Jews, and

[c] Matt. xvi. 21. Mark viii. 31. Luke ix. 22.
[d] Acts i. 7.

explain to them the fuppofed true and only great caufe of his death, but alfo that he keeps a profound filence upon this fubject in the general courfe of his preaching, and in his converfations with his Difciples, both before and after his refurrection: and further, that his Apoftles obferve the fame filence in all their addreffes and difcourfes, recorded in the hiftory of their Acts[e].

Here, again, the argument may with equal force be turned againft our Adverfary. For neither does our Lord, in any of his converfations with his Difciples, prefs upon them the neceffity of his own death, in order that, by rifing again, he may give a proof and example of a refurrection from the dead; nor do his Apoftles, in any of the places alleged, infift upon this as the great and only true caufe of his miffion. They indeed frequently appeal to his refurrection; but, as will prefently appear, it is for the moft part with a different view.

But I wifh not to dwell any longer upon this point; I would rather enquire whether a fatisfactory reafon may not be affigned for that filence, which is thus urged as an objection to our doctrine.

[e] Hift. of Cor. p. 161.

That

SERMON VII.

That there were many subjects upon which our Lord did not think fit to open himself, even to his immediate followers, while he was upon earth, he himself acknowledges, assigning at the same time the reason of his reserve. " I have yet," says he, " many " things to say unto you; but ye cannot bear " them now [f]." Men cannot bear that the whole truth should break in upon them at once; but must be gradually prepared for its reception. It is with the spiritual, as with the natural man : we are not in a state of infancy able to bear that strong nourishment which is proper and even necessary for us, at a maturer age : so there are mysteries belonging to the kingdom of God, which ought not to be unfolded, except to those who are come unto a perfect man, " unto the " measure of the stature of the fulness of " Christ [g]." St. Paul speaks of his Corinthian converts as in a state of childhood; and declares, that he had been obliged to speak unto them as unto babes in Christ, and to feed them with milk, and not with meat; for, says he, " hitherto ye were not able to " bear it, neither yet now are ye able [h]."

[f] John xvi. 12.   [g] Eph. iv. 13.   [h] 1 Cor. iii. 2.

The work of converſion and inſtruction is an arduous work, requiring the greateſt prudence and caution. The ground muſt firſt be cleared, and the foundation properly laid, before the building can be raiſed. In like manner the mind muſt be freed from antient prejudices, and be rightly inſtructed in the principles of the doctrine of Chriſt, before it can attain unto a perfect knowledge of the Goſpel. Our bleſſed Saviour well knew the temper of thoſe with whom he had to do; and what mode of conduct was moſt likely to prevail. His countrymen, to whom he principally addreſſed himſelf, entertained, as we have ſeen, falſe notions of Meſſiah's character; and their prejudices were ſo deeply rooted, that nothing ſhort of Divine authority ſeemed capable of removing them. Accordingly our Lord does not, immediately and at once, oppoſe to theſe prejudices the real nature of his miſſion, by declaring, in expreſs terms, the true end of his coming into the world: his aim is rather, in the firſt place, to convince them of the Divine authority with which he acted; and to gain their attention to his doctrine, by performing among them ſuch mighty works, as they muſt themſelves acknowledge

SERMON VII.

knowledge no one could perform, except God were with him. If, at his firſt appearance, he had, without any preparation, publicly declared the true end and deſign of his miſſion, he would have given univerſal offence to that prejudiced people; who, inſtead of hearing him gladly, would with one conſent have combined againſt him, as an enemy to their nation, and a blaſphemer of their God, without attending to, or perhaps giving him an opportunity of exhibiting, thoſe proofs of his miſſion to which he appealed. We therefore find him, at his firſt appearance, ſcrupulouſly endeavouring to conceal from the people his real character. The Devils, who knew him, he ſuffered not to ſpeak[i]: and after his immediate followers had confeſſed him to be the Chriſt, " he ſtraitly charged " them, and commanded them to tell no " man that thing[k]." The world in general was not as yet prepared to receive this great truth; the public declaration of which was reſerved for the Apoſtles, who, after the reſurrection of their Lord, were to be his witneſſes to the people. At preſent, therefore, the knowledge of the Saviour was confined

---

[i] Mark i. 34.   [k] Luke ix. 21.

to thefe chofen Difciples; and our Lord's more immediate care was to prepare them for the work to which they were called. But even to them he does not reveal himfelf openly, and at once; but leaves them, under the influence of the holy Spirit, to draw their own conclufion from what they faw and heard. And when at length their conviction drew from them the general confeffion above-mentioned, that he was " the Chrift of God," he fuffers them ftill to remain in ignorance of the true end of his miffion: nor was it till after his afcenfion into heaven, that their minds were fully illuminated with the knowledge of Divine truth.

Such was the prudence and caution obferved by our Lord, in revealing to his immediate followers the truths of the Gofpel. And the fame prudential conduct they, in their turn, obferved, in delivering to others the things which they had received. While our Lord was upon earth, his doctrine and miracles had fo far attracted the notice of the people, as to excite in them fome expectation of his being the great Deliverer, predicted by the prophets. But, ignorant of Meffiah's real character, and big with the hope of worldly power and grandeur, they were impatient

SERMON VII.

patient at the difappointment of their afpiring views, and turned with difguft and abhorrence from a crucified Saviour. To the Gentiles, alfo, the doctrine of the Crofs appeared no lefs unreafonable; and could not fail of expofing the preachers of it to their contempt and ridicule. Thus the preaching of Chrift crucified was " to the Jews a ftumbling-" block, and to the Greeks foolifhnefs;" and proved among both, the greateft impediment to the progrefs of the Gofpel. It was therefore the firft and immediate care of the inftructors of mankind, to remove this impediment, and to convince both Jews and Greeks, that the crucified Jefus was, notwithftanding his ignominious death, both Lord and Chrift; a Prince and a Saviour; the proper object of their faith, and the firm foundation of their hope. And as Jefus himfelf had formerly appealed to his miracles in teftimony of his Divine miffion; fo they, in confirmation of their doctrine, infifted upon that greateft of miracles, his refurrection from the dead; which they every where held forth, not fimply as the proof and pledge of our own, but rather as a moft convincing argument that he is very Chrift, advanced to the higheft ftate of power and glory,

and

and ordained to be the judge of quick and dead[1].

In this general manner did the Apoſtles preach the Goſpel to the unconverted: and of thoſe whom they convinced by their preaching, they required no other confeſſion than ſimply this; that *Jeſus is the Chriſt, the Son of God:* for their faith in this fundamental doctrine being fully eſtabliſhed, they would be difpoſed to lay aſide their former prejudices, and to receive, with meekneſs and

---

[1] See St. Peter's difcourfe to the *Jews* immediately after the deſcent of the Holy Spirit, Acts ii.; and again in the temple upon the cure of the impotent man, ch. iii; and to Cornelius, and the other *Gentiles* aſſembled with him, ch. x. See alſo St. Paul's difcourfe to the *Jews* at Antioch, ch. xiii; and at Theſſalonica, ch. xvii. Theſe all are among the places referred to by Dr. Prieſtley. The other places to which he refers are the following: The ſpeech of Stephen at his trial, ch. vii; the difcourfe of Philip the Evangeliſt to the Eunuch, ch. viii; St. Paul's difcourfe to the *Heathens* at Lyſtra, ch. xiv. and at Athens, ch. xvii; before Agrippa, ch. xxvi. and at Rome, ch. xxviii. But on no one of theſe occaſions does the ſpeaker profeſs to treat of the doctrine of Atonement, or of a reſurrection and a future ſtate, or of any of the peculiar doctrines of Chriſtianity: his deſign is rather to apologize for his own conduct; or to convert and bring over either the idolatrous Heathens to the worſhip of the true God, or the unbelieving Jews to a general confeſſion of faith in Chriſt.

ſubmiſſion,

SERMON VII.

submission, those other Divine truths, in which they should afterwards be instructed. So that the silence of our Lord in his conversations with his Disciples, and of these Disciples in their subsequent addresses to the unconverted, with respect to the doctrine of Atonement, appears to have proceeded from prudence and design; and to have been the necessary consequence of that mode of instruction, by which the truths of the Gospel were originally communicated. The teachers of religion were reserved only where reserve was expedient, and tended to the furtherance of the Gospel: on other occasions they opened themselves more freely. Even John the Baptist, after he had prepared his Disciples to receive our Lord as the promised Messiah, pointed him out to them under the character of " the lamb of God which tak-
" eth away the sin of the world [m]." And our Lord himself at the institution of the Eucharist, when now his Disciples had fully acknowledged him to be the Messiah, and their faith in him as such, was confirmed beyond danger of being shaken, speaks of his blood as being " shed for the remission of sins [n]."

[m] John i. 29, 36.   [n] Matt. xxvi. 28.

And

And in the Acts of the Apoſtles, that book, in which we are triumphantly told that not a word is dropped by any of the Apoſtles reſpecting this doctrine; in that very book St. Paul exhorts the Epheſian *Biſhops* to " feed " the Church of God, which he hath pur- " chaſed with his own blood º." And in his epiſtles to the ſeveral Chriſtian Churches whom he addreſſes, he ſhuns not to declare unto them the whole counſel of God; but infiſts (as do alſo the other Apoſtles) with no leſs freedom and fulneſs upon this, than upon any other undiſputed doctrine of the Chriſtian faith.

It appears, then, that the occaſions referred to by our Hiſtorian, were ſo far, as is pretended, from affording to our Lord and his Apoſtles an opportunity of diſcourſing, with openneſs and freedom, upon the doctrine of Atonement, that they rather required that ſilence and reſerve upon which the objection is founded. Conſequently this objection, like the others before conſidered, is without force, and falls to the ground.

We have now conſidered the principal of thoſe arguments, by which the Hiſtorian of

º Acts xx. 28.

the

the Corruptions of Christianity has thought fit to assail the doctrine in question. And I trust it must have appeared that nothing advanced by him is any real objection; much less of weight sufficient to justify the rejection of the plain and obvious sense of those numerous passages of Scripture, by which the doctrine is supported, in order to make room for that remote and figurative sense, for which he contends. And since the doctrine of Atonement is thus agreeable to the plain, untortured sense of Scripture in a variety of passages, and is no where irreconcileable with the language of the sacred writers; since it is perfectly consistent with the other acknowledged doctrines of our religion, and is in common with them freely insisted upon by the inspired penmen, whenever they judge it suitable to the occasion, and for the advantage of those to whom they addressed themselves; what shall hinder us from concluding, that it is part of that " faith " which was once delivered unto the " Saints [p]." Indeed, were the objections against it much more serious than we have found them to be, a doctrine, confessedly of

[p] Jud. 3.

such

fuch importance, ought not eafily to be refigned. But when in reality thefe objections are weak and frivolous, founded for the moft part upon mifconception and miftake, and at beft are fpecious rather than folid; with how much greater confidence fhall we preferve and keep it? To the followers of a vain and fceptical philofophy, conceited of their own knowledge, and trufting in their own righteoufnefs, the doctrine, for which we contend, may appear, as it did to the Greeks of old, mere foolifhnefs. But to the humble Chriftian, who takes the Scriptures for his guide, it is a doctrine full of comfort, and of hope. Senfible of the infufficiency of mere human virtue, he difowns all confidence in himfelf; and looks for acceptance, not on account of his own righteoufnefs, but for the fake and through the mediation of Jefus Chrift, who " fuffered for fins, the juft for
" the unjuft, that he might bring us to
" God ^q."

^q 1 Pet. iii. 18.

SERMON VIII.

Rom. iii. 25, 26.

Whom God hath set forth to be a propitiation, through faith in his blood, to declare his righteousness for the remission of sins that are past, through the forbearance of God; to declare, I say, at this time his righteousness, that he might be just, and the justifier of him that believeth in Jesus.

IT is the peculiar excellency of the Christian religion, that its doctrines are addressed not to the understanding merely, but to the heart also; and are all of them eminently calculated to affect the lives of Believers, and to promote the practice of piety and virtue. This is the acknowledged tendency of all the undoubted articles of our most holy faith; nor can any opinion, which has been generally received as a Chriftian doctrine, be more effectually degraded from its affumed rank, than by fhewing that it tends rather to produce the oppofite effect.

Upon this ground the doctrine of Atonement has been attacked and impeached. For while, on the one hand, the advocates of this doctrine affirm with confidence, that it has a moft powerful influence upon the practice of all who fincerely receive it; its opponents, on the other, no lefs confidently deny that it has any fuch influence : they rather infinuate that it has a pernicious tendency ; being, according to their reprefentation, fo contrived as to give the minds of men " unfavourable impreffions " of the Divine government, which, if not cor- " rected by fomething elfe, muft," we are told, " have an unfriendly afpect upon their virtue."

It is not my defign to enter upon a regular examination of the arguments adduced in proof of that pernicious influence, which is thus afcribed to our doctrine. I fhall only obferve, that they proceed principally upon the fuppofition that it reprefents the Deity in a vindictive point of view, requiring full and adequate fatisfaction to his offended juftice, and withholding mercy even from fincere penitents, till fuch fatisfaction be made.

Now

SERMON VIII.

Now it is infinuated[a], that, according to such a doctrine, God's moral government is founded upon a blind principle, whose only end is to obtain satisfaction for itself, which, when provoked, it craves indiscriminately of all that come within its reach, or that throw themselves in its way. But in opposition to such a blind principle of government, and such an unworthy end, our Author contends, that in the Deity *goodness* or *benevolence* (of which *justice* is asserted to be a mere modification) is the *sole* governing principle; and that its *only* object and end is the supreme happiness of God's creatures and subjects. Having thus stated that in God's moral government, the sole principle is goodness, and the sole end, the happiness of his creatures, he proceeds to argue, that whatever has not a tendency to promote the *end*, must be inconsistent with the *principle:* that in the all-perfect government of God, this end is not promoted by any severity shewn to *penitents* themselves; that therefore to exercise severity upon them is unnecessary; and to exercise it upon others, as, the doctrine of Atonement requires, is absurd. And this is the ground

[a] Hist. of Cor. v. i. p. 168.

upon which the doctrine of Atonement is aſſerted to give the minds of men thoſe unfavourable impreſſions of the Divine government, by which, if uncorrected, their virtue would be endangered.

In order to ſhew the weakneſs and irrelevancy of this whole argument, I need only briefly repeat what I have already diſcourſed upon at large. It has been ſhewn, that atonement means ſimply *reconciliation*; and therefore does not neceſſarily imply any ſatisfaction at all: conſequently the doctrine, conſidered generally, cannot be affected by an argument, the very baſis of which is *ſatisfaction to Divine juſtice*. It has been further ſhewn, that of thoſe who aſſert a ſatisfaction to Divine juſtice, the greater part mean not ſuch a rigid ſatisfaction as an offended perſon might be ſuppoſed to claim as a matter of right, and by way of compenſation; but ſuch as a prudent governor, anxiouſly concerned for the welfare of his ſubjects, might think fit to require, in order to maintain a reſpect for his laws, and to preſerve his authority from contempt. But the argument of our Hiſtorian proceeds upon the ſuppoſition of an *adequate* ſatisfaction, claimed by the Almighty Governor of the univerſe, ſolely upon his own account;

count; and is therefore wholly inapplicable to the doctrine of Atonement, considered under this view. Lastly, it has been shewn, that even they who understand *satisfaction* in its most rigid sense, still suppose that it was required in order to maintain the inviolability of the Divine attributes, that God might be merciful without prejudice to his justice. But from this opinion, it by no means follows, that satisfaction was blindly or vindictively demanded; on the contrary, we should rather infer, that the appointment of it proceeded from the Divine goodness or benevolence. So that under no view of our doctrine is there the least reason for asserting, that its Advocates intend any opposition between the justice of God and his goodness; or that they mean to set up a principle of government, which has not for its object the happiness of God's creatures. Thus this whole argument proceeds upon a misconception, and a false view of the subject: and the foundation being thus sandy and weak, the superstructure cannot but fall.

But while I thus contend, that nothing in the doctrine of Atonement, under any view of it, is really inconsistent with what is here proposed as the principle of God's moral government,

vernment, and the end which it has in view; let me not be thought implicitly to fubfcribe to the propofition itfelf in its full extent. For if I underftand it right, it in effect maintains, that the fupreme happinefs of God's creatures is the *fole* end of all the meafures of his government, and confequently that any meafure, of which this happinefs is not the primary and immediate object, cannot confift with his governing principle. Now that the meafures of God's government have all of them, through his goodnefs, a general tendency to promote the good of his creatures, I readily allow: but that the good of his creatures muft be the *fole*, or indeed the *great* and *primary* end of every meafure, I am not prepared to admit. The Scriptures feem to fpeak a different language: they affirm, that *the glory of God* is the great end of creation itfelf; and that the promotion of his glory is the thing principally intended by the whole courfe and order of the univerfe. " For of " him, and through him, and to him, are all " things: to whom be glory for ever [b]." " Thou art worthy, O Lord, to receive glory, " and honour, and power: for thou haft

[b] Rom. xi. 36.

" created

SERMON VIII.

" created all things, and for thy pleafure " they are, and were created [c]." Though therefore we fhould fail in fhewing that any difpenfation was immediately defigned to promote our own happinefs, ftill it would by no means follow that the difpenfation itfelf is inconfiftent with the general defign of God's providence. Far be it from us to fuppofe that always our good, and never his own glory, ought to be the immediate object of the meafures of his government. There may be in the nature of God fomewhat fo adverfe to fin, as to require the appointment of a propitiation. It may be that the glory of his attributes, of his juftice in particular, may be concerned in fuch an appointment: at leaft we cannot know to the contrary: and therefore it is not for us to reject a propitiation on account of its fuppofed inconfiftency, with what we may (ignorantly perhaps) affume as the fundamental principle of God's government.

But in the prefent cafe there is no fuch inconfiftency. For whatever might be the primary intention of a propitiation for fin, confidered generally, we fcruple not to affirm,

[c] Rev. iv. 11.

that the propitiation appointed for the fin of man, had in view the good of man : which, as I conceive, it effectually promotes, not only by procuring our deliverance from the punifhment of fin, and our reftoration to the favour of God; but alfo by its influence upon our conduct, derived from that manifeftation of the righteoufnefs or juftice of God, which is exprefsly afcribed to it by the Apoftle in the text: a manifeftation, calculated to fill the mind with fuch awful apprehenfions of the Divine Being, as muft have a direct tendency to promote repentance; and the practice of virtue. In the enfuing Difcourfe I propofe to elucidate the Apoftle's meaning, and to fix the true fenfe of the words before us, that we may be able to apply them with advantage to our prefent argument: and I the more readily clofe my labour with an illuftration of this important paffage, becaufe I conceive it affords a ftrong confirmation of the whole doctrine for which we have been contending.

In the chapter before us, the Apoftle is treating of man's juftification in the fight of God ; of which he propofes two methods: the firft is by our own obedience to the Divine

vine law; the works of which "'if a man " do, he fhall live in them ᵈ." This obedience he elfewhere calls " the righteoufnefs " which is of the law ᵉ:" and fince, if it could be attained, it would proceed from the exertion of thofe powers and faculties which God hath implanted in our nature, it is alfo called *our own* righteoufnefs ᶠ. The other method of juftification is by the grace of God, abfolving us from the guilt of fin, and not imputing our iniquities unto us. And becaufe this non-imputation of fin, for which we are thus indebted to the free grace and goodnefs of God, hath, as far as our acceptance is concerned, the effect of actual righteoufnefs, it is denominated, in oppofition to the former, " the righteoufnefs of " God." And, becaufe we apply the benefit of it to ourfelves *by faith*, or a firm perfuafion of the promifes of God, and a ftedfaft reliance upon his goodnefs, it is further called " the rightcoufnefs of God by faith."

Of thefe methods of juftification, the former is rejected by the Apoftle, as inapplicable to man in his prefent ftate of degeneracy and imperfection; fince he neither does nor can

ᵈ Lev. xviii. 5.   ᵉ Rom. x. 5.   ᶠ Ib. 3. ·

pay that ſtrict and entire obedience to the Divine law, which is required of all who ſeek in this manner to be accepted of God. " By the deeds of the law ſhall no fleſh be " juſtified; for by the law is the knowledge " of ſin." It remains, therefore, that we have recourſe to the other method, which is better adapted to the preſent condition of man. " For," ſays the Apoſtle, " all have " ſinned, and come ſhort of the glory of " God; being juſtified freely by his grace." And this juſtification the Apoſtle further declares proceeds to us, not immediately from God, but by the intervention of a Saviour. " Being juſtified freely by his grace, through " the redemption that is in Jeſus Chriſt."

Having thus laid the foundation of our acceptance in the mere grace and goodneſs of God, and declared the means by which it pleaſed God to carry into effect his gracious deſigns towards mankind, the Apoſtle proceeds, in the words of the text, to ſtate, that this Jeſus, in whom we have redemption, " God hath ſet " forth to be a propitiation through faith in " his blood:" " whom God hath ſet forth," ὃν προεθετο ὁ θεος; whom God propoſed, openly exhibited, or publicly announced " to be a " propitiation," to be the perſon in whom he

is

SERMON VIII.

is reconciled to finful man, and through whom he will accept as righteous all who by faith apply to themfelves the virtue of that blood which was fhed for the remiffion of fins [g].

The

[g] It has been obferved, that the word here rendered *propitiation*, in the original ἱλαστήριον, is the fame which is ufed in the Septuagint verfion, and alfo by the Apoftle himfelf in his Epiftle to the Hebrews (ch. ix. 5.) to exprefs *the mercy-feat*, that outward covering of the ark, above which, in the old tabernacle, God difplayed his vifible prefence to the Ifraelites. Hence fome Commentators have contended, that it ought to have the fame meaning in the paffage before us; which accordingly they render " whom God hath " fet forth to be a *propitiatory* or *mercy-feat.*" The *mercy-feat* was fo called, becaufe, under the Old Teftament, it was the place where the High-Prieft, on the feaft of expiation, fprinkled the blood of the fin-offerings, in order to make an atonement for himfelf and the whole congregation: and fince God accepted the offering which was there made, it may for this reafon be accounted the medium, through which God fhewed himfelf propitious to his chofen people. With reference to this, Jefus Chrift may be called a *mercy-feat*, as being the perfon, in or through whom God fhews himfelf propitious to mankind. And as, under the Old Teftament, God was propitious to thofe who came unto him, by appearing before his mercy-feat with the blood of their fin-offerings; fo, under the Gofpel-difpenfation, he is propitious to thofe who come unto him by Jefus Chrift, through faith in that blood (elfewhere called the blood of fprinkling) which he fhed for the

remiffion

SERMON VIII.

The intention, or defign, with which God was pleafed thus to fet forth, or openly to exhibit

remiffion of fins. (See Whitby's annotation on this paffage.)

But an objection may be taken againft this interpretation, upon the ground that it gives to the word ἱλαστηριον a mere declarative fenfe, making the Saviour entirely paffive in effecting a propitiation; and affigning to him no higher office than that of bearing teftimony to God's intentions towards mankind, or of declaring that the effect has been produced. Whereas the context, and full force of the paffage, feem to require that the word fhould be taken actively; fo as to afcribe to the Saviour an agency in propitiating God. Accordingly it has been contended, that the word fhould be rendered (agreeably to our own verfion) *propitiation*; fo that by ἱλαστηριον in this place, St. Paul is affirmed to mean that very thing which St. John expreffes by ἱλασμος; which latter word never fignifies a *propitiatory*, or that by means of which God fhews himfelf propitious; but a propitiation, or that on account of which he is become propitious; (fee Grotius de Satisfac. chap. vii.) and then the following words, " through faith in his " blood," ferve to declare both the means by which the propitiation was effected, viz. by the blood of Chrift fhed for our fins, and alfo the manner in which we are to apply the benefit of the propitiation to ourfelves, viz. by faith in the virtue and efficacy of that blood which was fhed.

There is yet another interpretation, of which the word ἱλαστηριον is capable: for (being deduced from ἱλαστηριος) it may fignify a *propitiator*, or the perfon by whom God is rendered propitious. (vid. Bezæ Annotat.) Taking the word bit the Redeemer as a propitiation, the Apoſtle ſubjoins in the words immediately following: "to declare his righteouſneſs for the re- "miſſion of ſins that are paſt, through the "forbearance of God." "To declare his

word in this ſenſe, we have here aſcribed to Chriſt the ſame office which the High Prieſt diſcharged, under the Old Teſ- tament, on the feaſt of expiation; that of propitiating God by an offering of blood; which blood, under the New Teſtament, is that of Chriſt himſelf, with which he en- tered, not, as the legal High Prieſt with the blood of bulls and of goats, into the Tabernacle made with hands, but into heaven itſelf, there to appear in the preſence of God for us, that all who believe in him may, by virtue of that blood which he offered, obtain pardon of ſins, and accept- ance in the ſight of God. And this third interpretation, while it is free from the objection urged againſt the firſt, in as much as it aſcribes to Chriſt an agency in producing the effect, and not a mere power of declaring that the effect is produced, does not, like the ſecond, take exactly in the ſame ſenſe two words which have indeed the ſame origin, but whoſe difference of termination ſeems to require ſome diſtinction in meaning.

But, in which ever of theſe ſenſes we take the word in queſtion, whether as a propitiatory, a propitiation, or a propitiator; whether as the medium through which God has declared himſelf propitious; as the thing on ac- count of which he is become propitious; or as the agent by whom he is made propitious; it cannot, I think, be de- nied, that the paſſage before us aſcribes to the blood of Chriſt a power of making propitiation, the effect of which we are to apply to ourſelves by faith. "righteouſneſs,"

SERMON VIII.

"righteoufnefs," εις ενδειξιν της δικαιοσυνης αυτȣ, for a *demonſtration*, or rather, *manifeſtation* of his *righteouſneſs* or *juſtice*. Juſtice, when applied to the Divine nature, is that attribute by which God, confidered as the governor of the univerfe, wills the puniſhment of thofe who tranfgrefs his laws. Confequently by God's demonſtrating or manifeſting his juſtice, we may underſtand his taking fuch meafures as prove to all the fubjects of his government the entire rectitude of his nature, and his invariable adherence to this eſſential branch of his character. Now the fetting forth of Jefus Chriſt to be a propitiation was a meafure of this kind, ordained by the all-wife Governor of the univerfe, to convince the world that he is a righteous judge, abhorring fin, and whatever appearances there may be to the contrary, entertaining a juſt feverity againſt it. I fay, whatever appearances there may be to the contrary: for that there were fuch appearances in the world, at the time of our Saviour's advent, the Apoſtle himſelf teſtifies in the words immediately following: δια την παρεσιν των προγεγονοτων αμαρτηματων; which our Tranflators have rendered "for the remiſſion of fins that are paſt:" but which, perhaps,

perhaps, may more accurately be rendered, agreeably to the reading of the margin, " for," that is, on account of, " the paffing over of fins " that are paft," or rather " fins which had " been committed before;" viz. before the time when God thought fit to give to mankind this manifeftation of his juftice. It is most certain, that in preceding times, before the coming of Chrift, God had paffed over fin, leaving it unpunifhed, or at leaft not punifhed as it deferved, and as his own threatenings, denounced frequently at the very time, and on the very occafion, feemed to require. I may inftance in that fin, to which the redemption that is in Jefus Chrift immediately refers, and in which we are all moft nearly concerned; I mean, the fin of our firft parents, in eating the forbidden fruit. Of the tree of the knowledge of good and evil, God commanded him, faying, " Thou fhalt not eat of it:" and againft the breach of this command he denounced fevereft vengeance. " In the day " that thou eateft thereof, thou fhalt furely " die [h]." The wifdom and goodnefs of the lawgiver force us to acknowledge, that both the command and the penalty were wife

[h] Gen. ii. 17.

and

and good: and his juftice might teach us to expect that he threatened not in vain, but would moft affuredly execute the fentence of the law upon the offender. But this was not the cafe: in the day that man finned, he did not die: on the contrary, he was allowed a further time of trial; and was left in the mean while not entirely void of comfort, or deftitute of hope. He was indeed denied the enjoyment of an earthly paradife; but he had before him the profpect of higher and more exalted blifs: and though, at the end of his day of trial, he was to quit this mortal ftate, yet his diffolution feems not fo much the *punifhment*, as fimply the *effect* or *confequence* of his former fin; and, with refpect both to himfelf, and to his pofterity, (who, being all partakers of his fallen nature, are with him·fubject to death) fhould rather be confidered merely as a paffage to another ftate of exiftence, in which, if they are not wanting to themfelves in this, they may be happy to all eternity. Thus was the fin of the firft man, againft which the penalty of death had been pofitively threatened, at moft only partially punifhed: and although, in after times, his pofterity had been guilty of the groffeft idolatry, and the moft flagitious de-

partures

SERMON VIII.

partures from their duty; yet God appears, in a variety of inftances, to have winked at thefe enormities, and to have fuffered men to proceed, after the imagination of their own vain heart, with impunity, and almoft without notice.

This paffing over of fin the Apoftle moft juftly imputes to " the forbearance of God:" and, in itfelf confidered, it is moft unqueftionably greatly to the praife of his mercy, and to the glory of his grace. But, on the other hand, it affords no manifeftation of juftice in the Deity; and might therefore be the occafion of men's entertaining falfe notions of God, injurious to his honour, and deftructive of their own welfare. Juftice, according to our natural conception, inftead of fuffering fin to remain unpunifhed, requires that vengeance be fpeedily executed againft an evil work. But if this awful attribute were perpetually veiled from the fight of men; if God continued to be filent when they committed fin, and fuffered them to go on without reproof, fparing when they deferved punifhment, and even heaping his benefits upon them; might they not be tempted wickedly to fuppofe that he is altogether fuch an one as themfelves; that juftice is no effential part of his character; on the contrary, that he views fin, not with indifference merely, but with approbation; and not only difregards the actions of men, whether they be good or bad, but even takes pleafure in wickednefs, and is not unwilling that evil fhould dwell with him? Or, if they proceeded not to fuch an height of impiety, might they not at leaft be led to build falfe hopes upon the mercy of God, which, they might imagine, would always triumph over juftice, and not fuffer him to reject the moft daring and obftinate offenders? And thus, in either cafe, the forbearance of God, inftead of leading men to repentance, would only harden their impenitent heart, and encourage them to greater degrees of violence and wickednefs. And therefore God, that he might remove all occafion of fo fatal an error, was pleafed to fend into the world his fon Jefus Chrift, in order to become the propitiation for our fins, and actually to make that reconciliation which had been ordained from the foundation of the world. And by thus publicly fetting forth and openly avowing the method of juftification appointed for finners, he hath fully vindicated his own juftice. For, being now affured that even the blood of the fon of

God

God was not esteemed too high a price to redeem the forfeited souls of men, and to save them from the curse and condemnation of the law, can we for a moment entertain a thought injurious to the character of God; or impute his forbearance of punishment to any weakness or defect in his nature? Shall we not rather confess, that, notwithstanding his passing over of sin, he is still a righteous judge; still concerned for the honour of his law, and attentive to the actions of men?

Before the coming of Christ, a propitiation for sin was not indeed entirely unknown. But being only obscurely promised, and faintly typified by the legal atonements, it could not illustrate in any great degree the Divine justice: and therefore the Apostle adds, " to declare *at* " *this time* his righteousness:" at this time; that is, now that Christ has appeared in the world. For whatever might be the case before; however the forbearance of God might hitherto have obscured his justice; yet after that Christ had actually appeared to pay the ransom, and to be the propitiation for sin, there was no longer any room for doubt. God could not now appear any otherwise than just, although he accepted, and treated as righteous, not those who, by a strict and entire obedience to his law, poffeffed in themfelves fuch an abfolute righteoufnefs, as gave them a pofitive claim to acceptance; but thofe who, though finners in themfelves, yet, by conforming to that gracious method of reconciliation which himfelf had appointed, poffeffed that other kind of righteoufnefs, by which juftification might be obtained; even the righteoufnefs of God by faith: " to de-" clare, I fay, at this time his righteoufnefs; " that he might be juft, and the juftifier of " him that believeth in Jefus."

The text, thus explained, applies without difficulty to the fubject before us, and affords a moft convincing argument, that the doctrine of Atonement is a practical doctrine, calculated to affect the lives, and to influence the conduct, of all who fincerely receive it.

For, in the firft place, the clear manifeftation which this doctrine affords of the righteoufnefs of God, is a moft effectual call to repentance.

No one, who thinks at all, could poffibly go on fecure in fin, did he not allay his fears by fome delufive hope, and encourage himfelf with a vain expectation of efcaping, in the end, the due reward of his deeds. Among the

the methods of deceit which men thus practife upon themfelves, there is none greater, or more frequent, than a dependance upon the Divine mercy. Upon this gracious attribute of the Almighty, all who prefer their fins to their duty, are apt prefumptuoufly to rely; and would fain flatter themfelves that it will fcreen them from vengeance in the day of wrath, and not fuffer them to fall into final condemnation. But let all who thus deceive their own hearts, confider with attention the method of reconciliation which God himfelf hath ordained; and they will foon perceive, that *the fetting forth of Jefus Chrift to be a propitiation*, takes from the impenitent finner every ground of prefumptuous hope, and teaches him the vanity of flying for refuge to the mercy of God, from the terrors of his juftice. For " if the righteous fcarcely be " faved;" if they who fincerely obey the Gofpel of God be redeemed from deftruction at fo dear a rate ; " where fhall the finner and the " ungodly appear ?" If the blood of the fon of God were not accounted too high a price to fave our fouls from death, and to make even penitent believers objects of mercy; who can for a moment imagine that impenitent finners will finally efcape the judgment of God?

He is indeed, as he proclaimed himself to Moses, a " God merciful and gracious, long-suffering, and abundant in goodness and truth; keeping mercy for thousands, forgiving iniquity, and transgression, and sin." But he is also, as he proclaimed himself at the same time, a God " that will by no means clear the guilty [i]." Although a God of mercy, he is still a righteous Judge; and hath demonstrated himself to be just, by the very method of justification which he hath appointed for mankind.

But, secondly, the effect of this doctrine is not confined to impenitent sinners. Such also, as willingly obey the Gospel of God, may be partakers of its salutary influence, and derive from it strength and support in the performance of their duty. For the setting forth of Jesus Christ to be a propitiation, while it demonstrates the justice of God, proclaims at the same time his abhorrence of sin, and tends to fill the mind with such awful apprehensions of his purity and holiness, as can hardly fail of exciting in us an habitual fear of offending him, and an earnest desire to " walk worthy of the Lord, unto all pleasing."

[i] Exod. xxxiv. 6, 7.

And

SERMON VIII. 231

And when we reflect, that, without shedding of blood, even the blood of the son of God, there was no remission, what a deep sense must we have of the evil of sin: and how must this consideration work upon us, to lament with godly sorrow the corruption of our nature, and the imperfection of our lives; to mortify our sinful lusts and affections; to watch over our conduct with care and circumspection; and, by patient continuance in well-doing, to approve ourselves to him who, by the very method of our reconciliation to himself, hath clearly manifested that he is of purer eyes than to behold iniquity.

Nor let it be imagined, as our Historian contends, that the doctrine of Atonement, admitting that it raises our ideas of the justice of God, must in the same proportion sink our ideas of his mercy [k]. The redemption of fallen man was, throughout, an act of mercy; and the method by which it was effected is so far from lowering in the least degree, that it raises this attribute to an astonishing height. That in our fallen state God should deign to look upon us, and, instead of rigidly inflicting the punishment due to our sin, should,

[k] Hist. of Cor. p. 170.

by the appointment of a propitiation, open a way to his favour, and again place within our reach life and happinefs; that without defert on our part, and even without folicitation, he fhould freely provide the means of our reconciliation to himfelf, and even when we were enemies, fhould fend his fon to die for our fins—can there be conceived greater love than this? or can any doctrine more powerfully vindicate, or more highly advance the Divine mercy? And thus the doctrine of Atonement is fo far (as it has been afferted) from lofing on the one hand what it may feem to have gained on the other, that it may rather be faid to gain on both. On the one hand, it demonftrates the juftice of God; on the other, it difplays his goodnefs, and exalts his mercy. And what additional motives are afforded, by this view of the doctrine, to the practice of piety and virtue! As well as to alarm the fears of the carelefs and unthinking, how admirably is it calculated to enliven the hopes of the humble and contrite; to confirm the faith of the weak and defponding; to inflame the love of the pious and devout; in a word, to put in motion, and give vigour to, all the fprings and principles of action, and thus moft powerfully to

engage

engage men to the practice of holiness here, by which alone they can secure to themselves a life of happiness hereafter.

But I need not dwell upon a case so plain. Enough, I trust, has already been said, to shew that the doctrine of Atonement is calculated to affect the lives and to influence the conduct of Believers; and consequently, that we do not without just reason urge its influence upon practice, as a strong argument in its favour. And with this argument I beg leave to close my illustration and defence of this important doctrine; subjoining only, by way of conclusion, a few general observations.

The purpose of God, in the dispensation of grace and mercy, which this doctrine unfolds to our view, was to rescue man from that wrath and condemnation, to which, according to the tenor of the first covenant, his disobedience had exposed him; and to place life and immortality again within his reach. To carry into effect this gracious purpose, God vouchsafed to ordain a propitiation for man's offence; in consequence of which the sentence of death, pronounced by the Divine law, was reversed; and this present life, no longer

longer a ſtate of innocence and enjoyment, was converted into a ſtate of trial and preparation; in which man is called upon to repent and turn from ſin, and, by a courſe of habitual and perſevering holineſs, to qualify and prepare himſelf for a life of eternal happineſs in a future ſtate. In the fulneſs of time it pleaſed God to ſend into the world his ſon Jeſus Chriſt; who, having taken our nature upon him, condeſcended to die upon the croſs for our ſins, and thus actually to become that propitiation which had been ordained from the beginning. By the ſanctifying influence of his blood he has conſecrated and purified his whole church; ſo that all who believe in him, obtain remiſſion of ſins; are juſtified in the ſight of God; are adopted into his family; and are permitted to approach his preſence with the confidence of ſons, ſure of finding a favourable acceptance, together with ſuch ſupplies of help and ſtrength as will enable them to finiſh their courſe with joy, and finally to attain that crown of everlaſting life, which is the end of their faith, and the object of their hope.

Thus, upon the reconciliation effected by the death of Chriſt, are founded all the mercies of this preſent life, and all our hopes of happineſs

SERMON VIII.

happiness hereafter. And this view of things is, as we have seen, clearly agreeable to the plain sense of Scripture, and to the obvious intention of the sacred writers. Should any man still be unsatisfied; and ask the reason of these things? should he enquire, why the shedding of blood was required for the remission of sins? why a simple declaration of God's will to receive sinners, upon repentance, would not have been sufficient, without an atonement? I am free to confess my ignorance, and hesitate not to say, I cannot tell. But let us not hastily conclude, that therefore no atonement has been made. Our very ignorance is an argument of the folly and danger of such a conclusion. Many things, at present concealed from us, might, if known, clearly evince the propriety, the expediency, the necessity of an atonement. Its propriety and expediency are in some measure manifest, notwithstanding our present faint and circumscribed view, from the glorious display which it makes of the Divine attributes, of the justice, the mercy, the goodness of the Deity; and from the beneficial consequences which this display is calculated to produce in ourselves. And who can tell what there may be in the pure and holy

nature

nature of God, which may make a propitiation even neceffary? God is omnipotent: but it is no impeachment of his omnipotence to affert, that he cannot do what is either abfolutely impoffible, or inconfiftent with his moral perfections. He cannot lie: he cannot deceive: it would be contrary to his nature to do fo. And who will fay that it is not equally contrary to his nature to pardon fin without a propitiation? This at leaft is certain, that we no where read of mercy fhewn to fallen creatures, upon any other ground. For fallen man a propitiation was appointed; and he became an object of mercy. For fallen angels no propitiation appears to have been appointed; and they are referved in chains of darknefs unto the judgment of the great day. Why thefe things are fo, fince God has not been pleafed to reveal, we do not prefume to fay, nor does it become us to enquire. It is not for us to penetrate the clouds and darknefs which furround the throne of God. It rather becomes us humbly to acquiefce in the Divine appointments; and whatever difficulties arife, or objections occur, to refolve them all into the unfearchablenefs of that myfterious excellence, whofe ways are not the ways of man. This one

one confideration, duly attended to, will teach us the vanity of being wife above that which is written, and of leaning to our own underftandings, in oppofition to the revealed will of God. It will rather teach us to receive with becoming gratitude that gracious method of reconciliation which God hath ordained, and, having received it, to hold it faft with unfhaken confidence.

And, that we may the more readily be induced to refift every effort of our adverfaries to undermine our faith, let us weigh with attention the danger to which fuch are expofed as depart from it. The cafe of apoftates is allowed to be defperate. " If any man " draw back, my foul," fays God, " fhall " have no pleafure in him [1]." And it behoves us to confider well, whether, by rejecting the doctrine of Atonement, we do not in fome meafure incur the guilt of thofe who apoftatize from the faith. " If," fays the Apoftle, " we fin wilfully after that we have " received the knowledge of the truth;" that is, if, after we have embraced the doctrine of Chrift, we again determine to reject and abandon it; " there remaineth no more

[1] Heb. x. 38.

" facrifice

"sacrifice for sins, but a certain fearful looking for of judgment and fiery indignation, which shall devour the adversaries. He that despised Moses' law, died without mercy, under two or three witnesses: of how much sorer punishment, suppose ye, shall he be thought worthy, who hath trodden under foot the son of God, and hath counted the blood of the covenant, wherewith he was sanctified, an unholy thing, and hath done despite unto the spirit of his grace [m]?" Let it be remembered, that this solemn denunciation of the Apostle is immediately subjoined to his discourse upon the Sacrifice and Priesthood of Christ, and may therefore well be thought to be nearly connected with it. And we may further observe, that he seems to place the great danger of apostacy in the privation of a sufficient sacrifice for sin, to avert the wrath of God. Now, though we do not absolutely tread under foot the son of God, yet if we deprive him of one of his essential characters; though we do not count his blood an unholy thing, yet if we esteem it worthless, and deny its atoning power, in what does our case essen-

[m] Heb. x. 26—29.

tially

tially differ from that of real apoſtates? Unclean and polluted with ſin, we dare not appear before God. But where ſhall we waſh and be clean, if not in the fountain of Chriſt's blood? He condeſcended to die for our ſins; and upon his death we may build the ſureſt hope of pardon and acceptance. But if we neglect ſo great ſalvation, what further ſacrifice for ſin remaineth to us? There can be no greater: there is no other. And if this be wanting to avert from us the Divine vengeance, what have we to expect but the judgment of an unreconciled God, and that fiery indignation which ſhall moſt aſſuredly devour the adverſaries of the truth?

Take heed, therefore, leſt ye fall into ſo fatal an error. But rather be perſuaded to hold faſt the profeſſion of your faith without wavering; being aſſured that " he is faithful " who promiſed [a]." So ſhall ye not be " of " them who draw back unto perdition; but " of them who believe to the ſaving of the " ſoul [o]."

[a] Heb. x. 23. [o] Heb. x. 39.

FINIS.

www.ingramcontent.com/pod-product-compliance
Lightning Source LLC
Chambersburg PA
CBHW031732230426
43669CB00007B/325